Jesus Loves To Heal Through You

ISBN-10:1530268214
ISBN-13:978-1530268214

For Worldwide Distribution, Printed in the U.S.A.

Jesus Loves To Heal Through You

My Personal Life Story of Victory over the Enemy and How to Walk Powerfully in Christ's Authority

Nelson L. Schuman

Dedication

To those in the world who have endured pain,
sickness, and disease or the suffering of loved ones

<u>Endorsements</u>

"Nelson has researched and is living out the truths of God's Word in the area of healing. These truths are for all to incorporate as they journey with Jesus. Nelson shares what God's unconditional love and grace has provided for us. This book will ignite a passion of hope for a deeper walk with Christ.

Owen Mason – Sr. Pastor, Church Alive,

Lafayette, IN

"I have always wanted to open up a Healing Room in the churches that I pastored but was never able to until God connected me with Nelson. He is truly a man of God that loves hurting people and helping them change from a life of pain to a life of gain. His healing anointing is truly miraculous and his heart for hurting people is amazing. He knows how to love like Christ loved the church and walk in His power and authority."

Tim Brown – Sr. Pastor, New Life Assembly of God,

Noblesville, IN

"I got to know Nelson by divine appointment at an overnight canoe trip. We spent all night talking, and soon after he sat under our school of ministry. He has the life experiences to teach others about God's healing power and is now operating under an extreme anointing from the Lord. I am honored to be a part of how God is using Nelson to set the captives free. He carries the authority of the believer with true humility."

David Natali – Sr. Pastor, Turning Point Ministries,

Carmel, IN

<u>Testimonies</u>

"I had suffered with a leg that was two inches shorter than my other leg. I met Nelson at a revival meeting in Ft. Wayne, IN and he worked with me for several hours showing me what God could do when we have faith. The enemy wanted my leg to be shorter than my other but I would not give up and after a tug of war for weeks I won as my leg is the same length as the other."

"I was born with a club foot as my right foot was a size (about an inch) shorter than my left foot. I had seen many people whose legs that were shorter grow out at church when Nelson prayed but had never seen a foot so asked if God could do that. Nelson immediately got excited and said 'yes I want to see that' so took me to the front of the church and prayed and immediately the foot started growing and in 4 minutes it was the same length as my other foot."

"My 7 year old son was battling non-Hodgkin's childhood Lymphoma for the second time in less than three years. The first time we went through the treatment process but it came back so were scheduled for surgery the next morning. I called Nelson the night before the surgery and over the phone he prayed 'lymph nodes be healed, cancer be gone in Jesus name' and instantly his neck got hot and the cancer dissolved. The doctor confirmed the cancer was gone the next morning. Thank you Jesus!"

"I had hurt my right knee a couple of days before coming into the Healing Rooms at New Life Assembly of God in Noblesville. Nelson prayed and the knee pain went away. Then I wanted him to pray for my severe knocked knees and instantly the knees moved outward to line up over my feet. Yay Jesus loves to do miracles!"

<u>Acknowledgements</u>

I want to thank my late grandmother Wilma Finch for handing me a book about the authority of the believer and praying for me to receive my prayer language as it changed my life radically from just a normal everyday Christian who never saw any of my prayers answered to one with power and authority that allowed me to do the same things that Jesus told us we could do. Grandmother, you always said you wanted a grandchild involved in ministry – the Lord gave you the desire of your heart and I am so blessed and honored to serve God in this way.

I also want to thank David Pierson for his expeditious time editing this book that will ultimately change the lives of countless people in this world from a life of pain to health. You are an extremely generous man of the highest integrity who loves the Lord with all your heart, soul and mind. We share a kindred spirit of sacrificing everything for the healing and restoration of all who have suffered in this world.

I want to especially thank all of my family and friends that the Lord has brought into my life who truly love me unconditionally and know my heart is to help people with all I am capable of through Christ. You are all so awesome and I love you for your support and dedication:

(Aggie, April, Ashley, Austin, Becca, Bill, Bob, Brandon, Brian, C, Carrie, Cindy, Charles, Chris, Chuck, D, David, Dawn, Duane, Elaine, Erin, Garry, George, Gina, Hannah, Keith, Jan, Jana, Jess, Jessica, Joe, John, Jordan, Judy, Julie, Larry, Luke, Marshall, Marvin, Megan, Michael, Michelle, Misty, Neil, Nick, Nova, Owen, Patti, Patty, Paul, Phil, Priscilla, Randy, Remon, Robia, Ron, Steve, Sue, Taylor, Todd, Trond, Tyler, and Tim)

Table of Contents

Introduction

In life we grow up and most of us hope for the best but as *Forrest Gump* once lamented "Momma always said, 'Life is like a box of chocolates….you never know what you're gonna get.' " If we are raised in a typical non-Christian family there is little or no faith for health or healing other than visits to the doctor or hospital. If something happened to your health, the only way of getting better was to go to the doctor and hope that he or she could "fix" you, provided you could pay the bill. Without medical intervention, you were given to a life of pain and misery until you die. If we are raised in a typical Christian family there is occasionally a glimmer of faith but most people are taught that God must sovereignly decide to heal so pray that He will heal you and wait to see if you get lucky.

Fortunately, I was raised in a Christian home that had some faith for supernatural healing. I never knew exactly how God worked or that there was a more effective way to see people healed – a much better way. It is somewhat of a conceptual challenge to understand that it is always God's will that we are healed. We wonder, is God in a good mood today? Is He having a good or bad day? Are we "good enough" to be healed from a significant sickness or disease? Most people are not taught the truth from the Bible concerning what Jesus taught about healing. Many pastors do not see instant healings when they pray for someone or they are among those with a sickness or disease in their own lives. They were never taught at seminary, Bible College, or continuing education on the subject of healing and if they were it was usually not completely accurate.

The Enemy does not want you to know the truth; divine health is your right as a believer, but only if you really know that you know that it is your right. What if your entire life you were never taught by the church, pastor, or priest about one of the greatest truths ever – that Jesus really meant it when he said in John 14:12 NKJV *"Most assuredly, I say to you, he who believes in Me, the works that I do he will do also; and greater works than these he will do, because I go to My Father."* How many believers today are actually doing the same or greater works than Jesus? Jesus began his ministry around age thirty with his first miracle of turning water into wine. The Bible states in Luke 3:23 NJKV *"Now Jesus Himself began His ministry at about thirty years of age, being (as was supposed) the son of Joseph, the son of Heli".* Jesus died on the cross, arose from the dead, and left the earth at age thirty-three after a total of about three years of ministry. I read John 14:12 to say that we should be able to do many more miracles than Jesus if only we are aware of and are actively exercising our authority for more than three years. If we are actively working to heal people for twenty or more years then we most assuredly will be able to see many more healings than Jesus ever did based on doing them over a much longer timeframe. How many persons do you know that have been healed, who are praying for people to be healed, or seeing consistent healings? Sadly the reality is that most people in this world do not see anyone healed nor do they operate in the same authority as Christ. What good is it to be a Christian on earth if we are as sick and hurting as those who are non-believers? Jesus did not die in order that we should continue to be sick and diseased and in fear the same as a non-Christian. There is so much more than only knowing that someday when you die you will hopefully get to heaven! My objective is to make everyone aware that if you are a believer in Christ you can live a life free from sickness and disease. In spite of many sicknesses and diseases that your father, mother or ancestors had for centuries, if you are aware that you have been given authority by Jesus Christ, you can get that revelation into your spirit and walk in that authority every day of your life. It is time to reexamine what the authority of the believer means and to walk in the same life-giving health as Christ. Miracles, signs and wonders will follow you all of your days!

Chapter 1

The Early Years

I was born January 2, 1967 in a small town west of Fort Wayne, Indiana named Columbia City in a hospital that my great, great, Uncle Dr. O.V. Schuman had agreed to have built by donating $50,000 (about $500,000 in 2016 dollars) to Whitley County. In order to build the hospital the county had to raise $50,000 in matching funds by a certain date and they just barely met the deadline. Prior to the new hospital being completed people had to go to the Wolf Lake hospital but in 1951 the Whitley County Memorial Hospital opened at last. Dr. Schuman was a caring man who once treated a man who had a farming accident and knew that the man was not well off so he only charged him 25 cents. Later someone mentioned to Dr. Schuman that 25 cents did not cover the cost of the bandages and gauze that he had used on the man. Dr. Schuman replied "Twenty-five cents is all that he can afford to pay – I would rather bill him twenty-five cents that he can pay and make him feel like a man than charge him more and make him feel like a deadbeat." I would like to think that some of Dr. Schuman's love and compassion for people was flowing through the Schuman bloodline to me as I feel the exact same way about loving and helping people that are in need or are hurting.

Another interesting fact about Columbia City, is that the greatest female healer in world history had started her healing ministry just blocks from where I grew up. Maria Woodworth-Etter was born July 22, 1844 in New Lisbon, Ohio (Columbiana County) and had been working in ministry for many years with the goal of converting non-believers into Christians. The Lord spoke to her and told her He wanted her to start healing the sick and diseased. She was not persuaded as she felt dealing with a lot of sick people would be more of a bother than she wanted. Finally relenting, she agreed to start praying for the sick on March 12, 1885 in Columbia City while having revival meetings at the Universalist Church and a skating rink. She lingered in Columbia City for four weeks conducting healings and seeing a great revival break out resulting in many converts. She was convinced that Jesus wanted her to heal people in order that they should become believers and no longer live in pain and sin.

I grew up in a house at 358 North Line Street which was just down the street from where Maria saw her first miracles. I never knew that was where she started her healing ministry until August of 2015 when I happened to sit next to Maria's great, great, great grandson, Jack Welch, at a meeting northwest of Muncie, Indiana. I talked with him at length and he said the past few years he was retracing the footsteps of her ministry. He had visited Columbia City recently and said that she at one time had meetings at the First Church of

God. Ironically as a young boy I was a regular attendee at the First Church of God in Columbia City and went to the nursery school while my mother played the piano and organ for the church.

Below is a picture of me with Jack Welch.

Also in 1918 Etter founded what is today Lakeview Church located on the west side of Indianapolis which I had attended a couple of times when my uncle and aunt attended. I also had engaged the church to host a dinner to raise funds for a missions program called *Light For The Lost*. It was incredibly astonishing to me to learn years later that my footsteps had crossed with Maria's and how highly anointed she was for healing people even though I had not heard of her name until 2009.

When I was five years old we moved our family from living in Columbia City to a 160 acre farm about 8 miles west near a very small town called Larwill (where my parents were married). We lived on a high hill and one winter as we were driving up the hill the car could not make it to the top. So we had to climb out of the car and try to pull ourselves up the icy hill. I fell and my leg was in the path of one of the tires as the car started to slide back down the hill and at the last second I was able to pull myself up and move my leg clear of its path. I was thankful to God that I did not lose or injure my leg (I have never suffered a broken bone in my lifetime). When I was in fourth grade I began to have issues with my throat and often becoming sick would miss school. In due course the doctor told my parents I would need to have my tonsils removed. I returned to the Whitley County Memorial Hospital and spent the night after surgery in December of 1978. I couldn't have known it was to be the 2nd and last time that I would step into a hospital needing any medical attention (the first being when I was born).

While living at our farmhouse my grandmother Wilma Finch from Lafayette, Indiana had prayed for me to receive the gift of praying in the Spirit (tongues) at age thirteen - which I received. My grandmother always wanted one of her grandchildren to be involved in ministry, but I knew that I would never be that person – or so I thought. I enjoyed attending churches when I was younger (Troy Presbyterian which was located north a couple miles from our farm) and some small Pentecostal churches in Warsaw and Columbia City before attending Calvary Temple in Fort Wayne, Indiana when I was a teenager. I never had any desire to ever be in ministry. I would read my Bible occasionally but never saw any miracles in my life. I knew that every now and then we would hear of someone being healed, but it was very rare. I believed God could heal people miraculously certainly, but never knew how or why it happened. I simply thought they were living a good life and God wanted to bless people with some healing every now and then.

When I was in my early teen years I had a bike accident that cut open one wart on my knee and it spread to become about twenty warts throughout my legs. I had to go to a clinic in Warsaw to have them removed. I will never forget what the Asian doctor said when I asked him how much it would cost. He told me $30. I was relieved to find out that all of my warts were only going to cost my dad $30 – what a deal. But then he said "No" – and began to point to each wart that he was burning off and said $30, $30, $30, at that moment I felt so bad that my dad was going to have to pay about $500-600 for all of them to go. I learned that day just how expensive healthcare is. I dreamed of the day I could avoid dealing with costly medical issues.

When I attended middle school at Pierceton I suffered from headaches and my mother took me to a chiropractor who determined that I had scoliosis (curvature of the spine). Subsequently, he began a regular treatment plan to gradually restore my back. It seemed to lessen the number of headaches but I was not permitted to play basketball my entire seventh grade year. I was sad since I was the starting center in sixth grade but was able to return to playing my eighth grade year.

I attended Whitko High School in South Whitley and was living a lukewarm Christian life. I listened to top 40 pop music, worked at Kroger in Columbia City, played basketball and was a regular at church. I never tried witnessing to anyone because I didn't have a "sold out" to God testimony to share in order to bring people to Christ. My mother was the strong spiritual influence in my life and she enjoyed reading books by Derek Prince, Kenneth E. Hagin, Bob Mumford, Kathryn Kuhlman and many others yet I never saw her walking in divine health. She suffered with aches and pains in her own life and was a proponent of taking vitamins and regular chiropractic care. Although mom prayed, I never heard her command healing like Jesus and her books said we should do. By graduation from high school my mindset was like most other Christians I knew. Healings are up to God, if you were good and He was in a good mood, so when you prayed you never expected to be healed instantly. When we would pray, we often times pleaded with God saying "if it be Your will please heal me" or something along those lines. I can barely remember anyone receiving healing and never instantly. Most folks would secretly live in silent fear of getting cancer or other life threatening health conditions, all while trying to retain our limited faith. I can honestly say I was totally clueless and ignorant of how walking in the health of Christ was at all possible. I put my faith in exercise, getting enough sleep, and avoiding sin so I would have a lesser likelihood of contracting some infirmity.

As a youth I remember watching a televangelist named Oral Roberts who appeared to usher in quite a few miracle healings at his church in Tulsa, Oklahoma. Also, they had cloths that were prayed over and mailed out for the purpose of remote healing, which was beyond my understanding. Dr. Roberts had people come to the stage and give their testimony of healing from cancer and other diseases. No one could explain to me, at a level I could understand, how it actually worked. Why are some healed and others not? What could be the determining factor for healing? I was curious but more puzzled than anything else. Youth are not typically concerned about health and I had mine. I only wanted to enjoy life and earn a good living.

In remembering Oral had prayed over cloths and sent them to heal people that were sick, I didn't recall this passage in the Bible where the apostle Paul had done that very thing. Acts 19:11-12 NKJV *"11 Now God worked unusual miracles by the hands of Paul, 12 so that even handkerchiefs or aprons were brought from his body to the sick, and the diseases left them and the evil spirits went out of them."* Incredible and amazing are the two adjectives that come to my mind! Years later I learned that a man by the name of Kenneth Copeland was a pilot that flew Oral Roberts around the country and he learned a great deal from his interactions with Oral. Kenneth went on to minister for many years himself. Essentially my remembrance of healing is that God may heal, but not anyone I knew individually.

Chapter 2

College Days

The fall of 1985 I began college life in Ft. Wayne at a school named IPFW (Indiana University, Purdue University at Ft. Wayne) where I drove about forty minutes each way to classes then worked at Kroger in Columbia City about 30-35 hours a week. IPFW did not have a football or basketball team at that time and so seemed much like a larger version of high school to me. I was blessed with several scholarships that paid for my college expenses but required me to major in agriculture. I did not intend to pursue a career related to farming. Having been raised on a farm doing a lot of hard work, I wanted nothing more to do with farming. Farming instilled a strong work ethic, repulsion of laziness, and an independence for which I am eternally grateful.

My spiritual life consisted of attending church at Calvary Temple in Fort Wayne with Pastor Paul Paino Sr. and fellowship time with Christians. I read my Bible occasionally but never felt desire to press deeper into learning more about God or develop a personal relationship with Him.

After my freshman year many of my friends decided to take classes on the main campus of Purdue University in West Lafayette, Indiana. I too decided to make the move to West Lafayette at Cary Quadrangle with my brother's former roommate, Paul Mesko from Minnesota, who was a counselor for that floor. I remember seeing Campus Crusade staff come to our floor early that semester. I was really not focused on the Lord, so I remained anonymous and avoided conversation with them. At that time I attended First Assembly of God in Lafayette pastored by Charles Hackett and while there, became acquainted with many other believers. I began to play volleyball that fall with my brother Keith and saw a girl that I thought looked cute. I never asked her out because I thought she was older since she ran with an older crowd.

During my sophomore year I determined to join a fraternity called FarmHouse, well known for being the tamest of the fraternities. Most of the guys were farm kids and several were Christians plus they were known as a house having a high grade point average. I remember participating as a pledge at the campus-wide singing competition paired with the women of Kappa Kappa Gamma. I will always remember the song we sang for the campus wide competition, "Let There Be Praise" by Sandi Patty. As a group we must have practiced the song at least 200 times, over and over and over for many weeks in preparation for the competition. To this day I still remember most of the words. I found it fascinating to be allowed to sing a Christian song on a public Big Ten university campus. Inside of me it felt encouraging singing positive words that uplifted everyone's faith. As it turned out we won the competition against about 20 other groups.

Through the singing competition, I met and befriended a very pretty girl named Stacy who was a little sister to one of the FarmHouse men. She drove a red sports car and occasionally attended First Assembly in Lafayette. During that time in my life I was being tested to see what kind of a Christian I really was. I would attend some of the weekend parties at FarmHouse and they would serve beer. I never liked the smell or taste of beer but forced myself over a couple of weekends to drink a few, even though it tasted disgusting to me. When I shared those thoughts with Stacy she told me "why do you drink something that tastes horrible to you?" I thought about it and determined the reason was to "fit in" with the crowd. I had never succumbed to peer pressure in high school and this was out of character for me. At that moment I became aware that fitting in to the crowd was not me, so I took the decision that day not to drink anymore. From that day forward I have never consumed another beer, and I have felt so much better for it! It is a blessing to have good friends that truly care about you as a Christian and can encourage you during times of weakness.

Ultimately after my sophomore year I knew that in my heart of hearts, I really had no desire to join the FarmHouse fraternity. I began dating the cute girl from volleyball at First Assembly. Throughout that summer I had my first real life crush. She was a secretary at First Assembly of God in Lafayette and would attend 6 am morning prayer. Since the girl I had an affinity towards did it – I decided I would as well. It was really difficult arising that early every week (we would attend once or twice a week) but my infatuation was my motivation. During this time, I learned a few things about praying but nonetheless did not consistently see healings, even though the Assembly of God church believed it was possible. As impressive as some of the prayers were, I never saw

God move in a dramatic way. This gave me no desire to pray for anyone to be healed and at the same time, I never heard the Lord speak to me.

We had a few prophets come to the church but I do not recall any who operated strongly in the healing gifts. I also do not remember hearing any pastor speak about how we carry the same authority as Jesus Christ to command sickness and disease from our bodies. I tried to live my life with limited sin and draw closer to the Lord but I never felt strong in the Lord in a way that was memorable for me.

By the time I was a college senior I was engaged to be married to the cute woman from volleyball. We were to be married December 30, 1989, about two weeks after graduation from Purdue, no small amount of pressure. Unfortunately one of my last classes was graded pass/fail – only one test at the end of the semester and if you earned a B or higher you passed, a B- or lower you failed. I learned prior to taking the test that on average over the past 5 years more than 60% had failed. The course was on personal finance, which I enjoyed. I received a passing 90%, graduated, and was able to get married on schedule.

Chapter 3

Married with Children

After marriage, we initially moved to the east side of Indianapolis to an apartment. We attended Calvary Temple on the east side and my wife worked as a secretary there. Once again I cannot remember a sermon that told me that Christians had the same authority as Christ to command all sickness and disease away. We moved back to Lafayette in June of 1990 and began attending First Assembly of God once again. We were soon expecting our first child, Jordan, and my wife gave birth March 2, 1991. I worked for a company called Bankers Systems out of St. Cloud, Minnesota and within a couple years became their top software sales executive out of sixteen reps across the U.S. I sold to banks and credit unions, loan and new account opening software to help their customers and members to complete forms that we created. I traveled around Indiana, Illinois, Kentucky and parts of Ohio as my sales territory. My walk with the Lord was minimal even as I attended church every Sunday and on Wednesday nights. I never heard from the Lord nor saw anyone healed or had any desire to heal anyone at all. I was asked to teach the college and career group at First Assembly and remembered that I had read a book on spiritual warfare and it talked about various demonic manifestations that took place in Africa. I was clueless about any demonic activities that took place in the U.S. or in Indiana in particular. I remember one interesting story in the book about a hula hoop-like ring that was rolling by itself on the ground somewhere in Africa being moved by a demon. That was the extent of my remembrance of that book and my knowledge of the demonic.

Our second son Austin was born September 18, 1992 and my career with Bankers Systems was flourishing. As more money was earned, I was able to buy a new car every three years as I was driving about 50,000 miles every year. Our daughter Ashley was born August 17, 1994. I started teaching Royal Rangers at First Assembly in Lafayette and we drove back and forth an hour each way for about a year before shifting to attend Northview Church in Carmel where I taught the Royal Rangers program that they were using. My Christian walk was still basic as I rarely felt I ever heard from the Lord but tried to live a high-quality life and love people the best I knew how. I would pray in the spirit from time to time but not regularly and I would read my Bible every morning. I never had a desire to pray for anyone to be healed because I had no clue how it worked and had not yet seen anyone instantly healed my entire life.

I was asked by Joe Livesay Sr. from First Assembly Church in Lafayette to lead their *Light For The Lost* missions steak dinner fundraisers every fall which I did for several years all across central Indiana. Almost 100% of the money that was raised at these steak dinners during a week in the fall went to produce Christian literature for multiple countries around the world. *Light For The Lost* organized to invite people from other Assembly of God churches to come to one larger church that would host the dinner for one night. Attendees would pledge to give money to fund the next year's mission teams. I had a hard time getting pastors at smaller churches to encourage their people to attend these events at a "competing" larger AG church. It was a difficult task because churches in Indianapolis seem to be more protective of their membership, only wanting them to attend their home churches.

Once in the late 1990's I was asked by Joe to attend a national *Light For The Lost* convention that was to take place near Orange County, California. I agreed to go and enjoyed the warm temperatures in the spring, played in their golf tournament, and also played tennis with a good friend named John Thompson. Unfortunately I breathed in some kind of virus because by the end of the convention, as I was playing tennis I started to cough up blood. This was strange and of course very concerning since I had never had any lung issues. As I flew back to Indianapolis I began to feel weaker and weaker and when I arrived late at night I barely had enough strength to walk to my car in the parking lot. I made it home and woke up the next morning to go to work but I could not get out of bed because I was so weak. I made an appointment with my doctor (Dr. William Kirsch) in Noblesville, Indiana and he ran x-rays on my lungs and determined they were 75% filled with liquid and I had pneumonia! He said that I would have died if I had waited another day to see him. He said typically I would have been hospitalized but they were going to prescribe antibiotics which should work well since I was healthy otherwise. Within a week I was back to normal. Dr.Kirsch told me something that has stuck with me long after that episode. He said "Since you caught pneumonia you will now be susceptible to have bronchitis and pneumonia for the rest of your life." Sure enough every year after that, I caught bronchitis (and pneumonia one time again) and had to take Zithromax® pills for a week to be cleared of it each time.

One day my wife and I were visiting my grandmother Wilma Finch at her home in West Lafayette. She was intrigued by various deliverance and healing ministries. Persons of whom I had no desire to learn about since I thought some of the beliefs were just plain weird. Kenneth Hagin, Derek Prince, Kathryn Kulhman, Oral Roberts, Benny Hinn and others were among her interests. She handed me several books, one of which was called *The Believer's Authority* by Kenneth E. Hagin. She had written an inscription inside of it that said "All the great men of God have this book as a part of their library." I took the book from her and promptly forgot about it. I never intended to read it, not one time, as I had no desire whatsoever. Little did I realize its future value and what that book would mean to me in my life many years later.

On Friday, August 22, 1997 I drove my family to visit my mom and dad and siblings Jana and Chris at the farm where I grew up. We decided to camp out on the farm thinking it would be fun for our kids to enjoy their first campout in a tent. On my drive up that Friday night my mother had complained of feeling numbness in her arms. The next morning I spoke with her and ate breakfast and then went back out to the tent. Shortly after I was outside my sister Jana ran out and anxiously told me something was very wrong with mom. When mom talked she was not making sense and Jana looked very scared. I ran back to the house and saw my mom with her head down on her arms at the kitchen table and she appeared to be crying softly. So I prayed in the spirit over her as I did not know what else to do and within a few minutes she stopped crying. Then I realized she had actually stopped breathing. I put her on the floor and called 911 and then began mouth to mouth trying to resuscitate her. She was gone before I started, having suffered a major heart attack at age 55. I had the grievous job of notifying all of my siblings that our mother had gone to be with the Lord. I cried off and on for many months after that and soon realized I needed to make sure my own heart was healthy. I arranged a stress test through my doctor. I committed myself to get into better shape and became really motivated to exercise.

I began running half marathons and eventually marathons (26.2 miles). I ran five marathons over the next 6 years including Chicago, Detroit, St. Charles (Missouri), Columbus (Ohio), and a practice marathon near home in Noblesville. I really enjoyed running and took AdvoCare workout supplements to help me run faster and have greater endurance. I was never the fastest in the largest marathons but do remember the time I ran a half marathon near Champaign, Illinois where my good friend Mark Daly from Bankers Systems rode his bike along the road near me to cheer me on. I finished 3rd in my age group out of about 60 runners which was breathtaking for me. Unfortunately a year later Mark learned he had a brain tumor and died within a year. I so wished I knew how healing worked back then! I could not help Mark even though I prayed for him many times in the best way I knew how. I was yet to learn about my authority from the Lord as a believer, for protection from sickness. I ran and trained for marathons thinking I would live longer due to the effects of exercise to strengthen my heart.

Meanwhile, my eldest son Jordan experienced a traumatic life changing event at the tender age of eight. A boy a year older who was living in our neighborhood in Noblesville did something to him that was not appropriate. It changed him dramatically from a boy who was happy, excited and loving, into a boy that was angry, defiant and would no longer allow me to hug him. We suffered through Christian counseling with no improvement as he went from bad to worse. He would say callous and disrespectful things to me and his mother and pick on his younger siblings. He also became obsessed at playing video games. Eventually we tried to limit him but he would always defy our rules and sneak to play them over and over. We had to hide the games and it was always a point of strife for our family. As Jordan became older he became more and more defiant and more out of control. He was a very good athlete and was one of the best pitchers at the Noblesville Youth Baseball league making the All Star travel team each year. Unfortunately he also became more rebellious and would not listen to me or his coach when we tried to give him guidance. He sometimes sneered or glared at the head coach causing friction due to his disrespect. I felt hopeless as a father because I never behaved that way when I was his age. I was always respectful and loving of everyone so it made me feel like a horrible dad for not being able to cajole my son to behave in a like manner.

As Jordan became a teenager, his behavior became more aggressive and he turned more violently against us. Managing Jordan was hopeless as he controlled the whole family and began telling us what to do. A father being ordered by his son is demoralizing and humiliating. The family lived in horrible strife due to one child that was out of control and no Christian counseling was effective. I felt as if I was wasting thousands of dollars every year while the doctors simply prescribed ADHD medication (Straterra®) for him. The drug caused stomach pain and his already limited appetite lessened and his skinny body became like a rail. I finally had to take him off of the drug. The counselors had no clue how to fix our son who was damaged through no sin of his own. The striving became worse and worse every month and year. When he was at school I was able to have peace but as soon as I heard the Noblesville school bus approach our neighborhood, I knew that our peace for the day was about to end and all hell would break loose. My stomach would become queasy and as soon as the door opened to our home the fighting would begin. Jordan would provoke his younger brother and sister almost immediately and while I was working upstairs in my office I would hear "Dad!" and have to come down and try to control an out of control boy who was quickly approaching manhood. I thought about placing him in an institution that could possibly help troubled boys, but I did not have peace in my spirit as I loved him and wanted to protect him. It was agonizing for me because on one hand my life was a living hell with him every day and on the other hand I would have felt like I was giving up on my son and I would miss him terribly. I felt as though I was the tormented one.

Meanwhile, on February 23, 2005 I was on a business trip in the Upper Peninsula of Michigan for the first time in my life. There was snow piled up everywhere as they usually received several feet of snow at one time in season. I was in a banking partner meeting and my phone rang from my brother Duane but I could not take it so I hung up. Then he called again and I hung up again. Then he tried again and I turned my phone off. After the meeting was over I called him but there was no answer. Then I called my wife and she said a police officer wanted to talk with me. I was scared to death that it was my son Jordan out of control once again. He could have committed any act or crime hurting himself or others and I would not have been surprised. The officer asked me if I was sitting down. I was in a restaurant somewhere in Upper Michigan and sat down by the restrooms bracing myself for him to tell me that my son was killed. He told me my father had died of a heart attack (he was 67) and I remember feeling so relieved that it was not my son. After the call I felt grief that at 38 years of age I no longer had a father or a mother. Both parents died by heart attack and I wondered how many years I might have before I might succumb to the same illness. I flew home thinking what I was going to say at the funeral. I still have the notes in one of my suit coat pockets. I was determined that I would continue to run in order to stay healthy but my spiritual life was not much more than going through the motions – attending church – teaching youth Bible stories – and trying to keep my family afloat as my son Jordan became more out of control every month.

I felt so hopeless as a father even though I was making over $130,000 a year but no money in the world could get Jordan delivered of his torment. I was willing to pay anything to get him healed and to have peace in my life.

Eventually with the strain of Jordan's issues on our already tenuous marriage, my wife decided to file for divorce in April 2007. I tried to slow or stop the divorce from moving forward as long as I could. My son Jordan learned that he could take greater advantage over our family by leveraging me against his mother. One time he would not listen to me as I tried to get him to stop making fun of his brother who was playing a video game in my bedroom. I tried to get Jordan to leave but he refused and in the end punched me on the chin several times. I held him in a bear hug and took him down to the floor then had my son Austin call 911. My daughter Ashley was also present and saw what had happened. The police arrived and I debated pressing charges and having him put in juvenile. Jordan was crying and appeared to have realized that he had crossed the line so I did not press charges. I told his mother but she just blamed me instead of supporting me which was very hard to take because I did nothing wrong. This became an invariable theme of my life over the next several years trying to help people who did not behave as they should, blaming me when I did nothing wrong other than loving them. Unfortunately, the divorce became final in June of 2008 and I remember thinking that my son's future was now doomed as he would either end up in jail or dead by the time he was 20 years old.

Jordan was 17 years old when he was fired from his first job at Kroger due to not showing up on time if at all. The divorce limited me from trying to force Jordan to do what was right. I was at the end of my rope and I felt so helpless to find the help he needed. During that same time I was trying to keep my daughter Ashley from becoming depressed. Ashley had a desire to pursue acting, modeling, singing or dancing so I enrolled her in a local school hoping for something positive. One day an agent from Hollywood came to Indianapolis and signed her to a contract.

Ashley was almost 14 at the time and she and I traveled to LA ten times during 2008. She had several auditions for shows like Disney's Wizards of Waverly Place and several commercials. It was an uplifting positive experience for both of us during a tumultuous and terribly sad period of our lives.

My spiritual life during this time was quite meager as I continued to attend East 91st Street Christian Church in Indianapolis but never heard from the Lord. I do remember telling Him that I would gladly give up all of my assets (at that time $500,000) and job (now making over $150,000 a year) if I could only have peace. At the time I was working for Intuit, a Mountain View, California company who had acquired Digital Insight, a Calabasas, California based company which was the leading internet banking software system for banks and credit unions in the U.S. I managed partner relationships for the largest core processors in the U.S. that maintained all the data for banks and credit unions and traveled around the country attending banking conferences. I also was able to mostly work from home and had a lot of flexibility with my time.

In October of 2008 The Lord started to draw me closer to Him as I sensed he wanted me to begin looking for my next wife because there was someone He wanted to connect me with who would take me into ministry. In fact I felt a desire to look for my next wife and had started to correspond with a few women online. I subsequently met a woman on a Christian dating site called Christian Café and we eventually met December 19, 2008 in Avon, IN. Almost immediately, I was quickly led into a spiritual transformation that changed my life forever. I began to hear the Lord speak to me on a regular basis for the first time in my life and my life was eternally altered. I started to sense things I had never felt and the Lord changed me into a much Godlier person than I had ever been. I had no desire to do anything but what the Lord instructed me to do, no matter the cost financially or emotionally.

Chapter 4

My Spiritual Awakening

The first week of January 2009 changed my life in such a dramatic way there is nothing to explain it other than it was all God. I was invited to attend a Christian conference that lasted almost a week at the Gaylord Opryland Resort in Nashville. An international evangelist from San Diego named Morris Cerullo was holding a conference that included a few people I had heard of: John Hagee, Benny Hinn and Myles Munroe among others, as well as a new young Christian singer named Britt Nicole. The first night there, when I raised my hands to worship to a song, my left hand began to shake uncontrollably. I knew it was God's doing because I was not making it shake and I knew it was a good thing as I felt the presence of the Lord like I had never felt it before. A few songs later my right hand started to shake along with my left. I knew it was a God thing and I thought it was so cool because I could not make them move that fast back and forth in the natural and I could feel the presence of the Lord all over me for the first time in my life. The woman that had invited me to come with her noticed and asked what was going on and I told her it was the presence of God even though I had never experienced that before in my life.

A day after we arrived at the conference, we were asked to serve together at a book table for the Morris Cerullo World Evangelism (MCWE) ministry. People asked us if we were married which felt strange because we had only known each other a few weeks but at the time it did feel in the spirit that we were going to be married soon and help other people. The second night of the conference we were moved to sit in the 2nd row, front and center with all the dignitaries and those that had given a lot of money to the ministry (there were about 3,000 people from around the world that were attending the conference). Then when I began to worship not only did both of my hands shake but my left and then right legs started to shake. It was amazing because this had never happened before yet I knew that it was God doing a work in me. Then people told me one of the days that they could see a large angel standing on my shoulders and I had felt the presence of the Lord very strongly on me during that time.

I began to hear from the Lord clearly – one of the first nights I walked up front at the end of the service and was standing behind the woman that I came with. The Lord spoke to me very clearly saying "You will love her like Christ loved the church" and I remember thinking 'who can do that?' and 'what does that really mean?' Then others came up to us that did not know us and told us that we were going to be married and have a ministry traveling all over the world helping hurting couples and youth through a very strong healing, deliverance and prophetic ministry. It was truly an amazing week in every way that changed my life forever. I felt as if I had gone through a heart transplant and was ready to do the Lord's work and become all that He wanted me to be. I donated over $20,000 to the MCWE ministry that week because I wanted to invest in the Kingdom of God and not myself any longer. I no longer wanted to amass over $1 million dollars for myself – I wanted to help hurting people and love on them to make their lives better and give them hope as I now had the heart of Christ inside me. It was the most amazing week of my life at that time and I was now on fire for God!

On January 19 (just one month after we first met) the woman and I became engaged in front of her parents and niece at the home she grew up in west of Indianapolis. A few weeks later we attended another Christian conference held by Judy Jacobs at the Gaylord Opryland resort. At the conference was a prophet named Glenda Underwood Jackson who was the great niece of one of the greatest healers of all time, Maria Woodworth-Etter (the woman who began a healing ministry in my hometown). I felt led by the Lord to meet her and to receive a word from the Lord from her as she said every word she heard from the Lord would come to pass and she only spoke what the Lord told her to say. She told us we were going to have a "marriage made in heaven and it was ordained by God" and that "we would travel all over the world helping hurting couples that were considering divorce and in strife and also help children to be at peace and heal a great many people and deliver them from demons." This was more confirmation of the words that we received when attending the Morris Cerullo conference just weeks before. Prior to arriving at the conference the Lord told me that we would learn when we were supposed to get married and the 2nd night we met a man named Jon Potter who had a ministry in Birmingham affiliated with Judy Jacobs was led to come to us and ask about our story. We told him how the Lord wanted us to get married but we did not know the exact date. We knew we would find out when we attended the conference that weekend. Immediately he heard a date from the Lord and said he never hears dates from the Lord. He said he heard the date of March

19th. At the time it was January 31st. So we prayed about it and the Lord said He did want us to marry on March 19, 2009 which was just over 6 weeks away. We hurriedly looked for a pastor to marry us but none around Indianapolis would because they did not know us both long enough. So we approached my friend and pastor Owen Mason from Church Alive in Lafayette, Indiana who had married my first wife and me and he said he would only agree to marry us if we would take tests at Emerge Counseling Services in Akron, Ohio to see if we were compatible. We told him about all the confirmations from people that the Lord wanted us to get married and we would have a powerful ministry to help hurting couples and others. The Lord told me that our testing would come back very similar and sure enough the results showed we were very close so Owen agreed to marry us.

We were married March 19, 2009 at the Indianapolis Country Club on the west side of Indianapolis and had about 75 people in attendance. We traveled to the Great Smoky Mountain National Park near Gatlinburg, Tennessee for the first part of our honeymoon and then to the Hotel Del Coronado on Coronado Island just off shore from San Diego for the second part of the honeymoon. I started to learn more about spirits and how they affect people as I felt led to read a book called *I Give You Authority* by Charles Kraft on our plane ride out and back. My son Jordan was still a mess and would be very hard to work with as the spirits afflicting him caused him to be very defiant, argumentative and even violent. In June of 2009 we started receiving ministry from an extremely anointed man from Torrance, California. He had a very powerful ministry teaching people their authority in the Lord and to hear from the Lord very clearly for direction. He also assisted healing people who were deeply hurt by people in their past (father and mother wounds) and launched them into their own ministries. On the second phone call he explained to me that my son wanted to be set free from the torment of spirits that had entered him when he was afflicted by the boy in our neighborhood in 1999. I told him that I never would have guessed that he wanted to be delivered because he seemed to really enjoy making my life miserable - he had punched me, disrespected me verbally all of the time, provoked arguments with his siblings, etc. He explained to me who my son really was and said he was a lot like me – loving, kind, gentle and patient and would be used in ministry to reach people that had received similar hurts. Those adjectives would never have been anything I would use to describe Jordan. Then he told me I had authority as a Christian but I never knew my authority because no church leaders told me about it. The Christian counselors I paid thousands of dollars over 10 years to help my son also did not have a clue about how to set Jordan completely free and heal his spirit. He explained I only needed to say an effective prayer over him and command the evil spirits to leave, and they would go instantly and Jordan would become changed forever.

About a week after I was told I had authority over evil spirits I decided to give it a try. My wife and I picked Jordan up in my SUV after we found him involved in things he should not have been doing and drove him back to our house in Noblesville. As we were parked inside the garage we asked him if we could pray for him. To my shock he actually said yes. So we held his hand and said a brief prayer that included "I command that all spirits not from the Lord be gone in Jesus name." He actually thanked us for praying and then went into the house. I could not tell if the command worked because he seemed the same as before with no noticeable change. But the very next day something amazing happened that I will never forget for the rest of my life!

I was mowing the grass at my house in the backyard and noticed Jordan walking toward me. I was bracing myself for another demanding, wicked comment to be made by him so I shut the mower off and waited for him to utter words that would be hard to hear for the millionth time. Instead I heard him say "Hey dad, can I finish mowing the grass for you?" I nearly fainted. Literally! I was in shock and had never before heard those words from his mouth. He had not even mowed the grass for at least the previous 18 months and if he did mow I had to pay him and plead with him several times because he would rather argue. I acted like nothing was out of the ordinary and said "Sure" and I let him start the mower and begin mowing while I carefully kept my balance from falling over and walked into the house. Once inside I stopped in the living room and fell to my knees and just started crying like a baby thanking God for delivering my son after 10 years of hell for him, me and our family. The Lord told me that now I would see who my son really was and he would become more like me every week and lose his selfish and mean ways and become loving, caring, patient and gentle. I was in shock for the rest of the day and sure enough Jordan became a different person overnight as he actually would allow me to talk with him and would listen and no longer act like he knew it all, ending all disrespect right then and there. Demonic spirits are real and do not let anyone ever tell you differently!

Over the next couple of months his appearance began to change as well. He once looked like what the children would call "Emo" wearing dyed black hair, gauges in his earlobes and every so often, larger gauges to stretch his earlobes further and further. One day his earlobe tore and just dangled for several weeks until Burger King (where he was employed) told him to fix it. His local doctor could not fix it and recommended a plastic surgeon which cost $700 to correct (then as Jordan started to get promoted into management they asked him to take out his other gauge and get it fixed, so another $700 lesson). Jordan also would wear mostly black clothes and tight, skinny skateboard-type jeans, but soon he began to wear more normal colorful clothes and less restricting jeans. It was an amazing transformation to witness first hand.

I finally got my son back from the enemy after 10 years of suffering every day with no hope in sight from the medical profession or those in the Christian counseling world because they did not know how to command demons out of a person or much less believe in them. My mentor told me that Jordan had the spirits of Malice, Divination (witchcraft), and Pharmakeya (from the stronger ADHD drugs) and they all were gone after I said the prayer over him in the garage. The Lord told me that this would be a significant part of my ministry because very few people in Indiana worked in deliverance ministry and the Lord was going to use what the enemy meant for evil for everyone's good in not only the state of Indiana but all over the United States and beyond. That was why it took so long for Jordan to see deliverance because the Lord wanted me to know what it felt like and to see what demons could do to a boy so that it was not just a blip on my radar screen. It was burned in my memory seeing how horrible the spirits could make a human being behave. Once he was set free, I would see him blossom into who he really was in Christ and it would be a beautiful thing for all to witness.

The Lord said that many other people who are anointed by Him are going through similar seasons and as long as they do not give up, the Lord will see it through. Your pain can become your passion and ministry. If we never have any hardships to overcome, how can we effectively minister to someone who is experiencing what we have never seen? There is something about having to endure tribulation for a time, sometimes for many years, that makes such an indelible mark on us for the rest of our lives. We are shaped and molded by what the enemy meant for evil. It causes something to rise up inside, to have a ministry borne from experiences that reading a book simply cannot replicate. If you have walked in the shoes of hardship you will command an audience of believers. People will quickly realize you know what you are talking about because you have been there, done that, and overcame! Glory to God you are now on the other side of that trial. So while it is never enjoyable suffering tribulations and even abuse, once you are finished with that season of life, the blessings that can come out of it are amazing and enormous. As long as we are longsuffering like Job and don't complain against God, He will take what the enemy meant for evil, and bless us. Look at tribulation as learned lessons that are shaping you into the man or woman of God that He called you to be. What does the Bible say about this? James 1:2-4 NKJV says; *"2 My brethren, count it all joy when you fall into various trials, 3 knowing that the testing of your faith produces patience. 4 But let patience have its perfect work, that you may be perfect and complete, lacking nothing."*

I told the Lord that I wanted one of the greatest testimonies the world has ever known. I knew I would have to endure some extremely difficult trials and much suffering in order to have a powerful testimony. But I always said that my pain would become His gain. I give all glory and honor to God for allowing me to willingly die to self and live with those who were extremely hard to love, while learning they were behaving out of pain that the enemy had inflicted on them through other people.

I remember crying about the story of my son for the next several years every time that I showed Jordan's picture of what he once looked like and what he looked like 2 years later. I knew the struggle we went through together and now no longer had to endure the strife since becoming free. The Lord told me to show those pictures to as many people as possible in order to provide parents hope for their own children that if He would do it for me He would do it for them. I must have shown his before and after pictures on my phone at least 1,000 times in the past 7 years. God was directing my ministry every time I would plant those seeds of hope. Every time I explain the miraculous transformation of my son, it brings a tear to my eye. Although he was no fun to be around while he had the spirits on him, it was worth every ounce of pain we endured because now I have my son back. We have an amazing testimony of God's goodness and why it is so important to teach people about their authority in Christ. The Lord also told me someday I would begin showing the before and after pictures of my son on the big screens at churches when I spoke about our story. That came to pass in January of 2016 at New Life Assembly of God in Noblesville. The photos show what a person can look like when they have demonic oppression present versus when they are completely set free. You can see the despair and hopelessness in the eyes before Jordan is set free and after deliverance there is a sparkle in his eyes.

Following are the before and after pictures of Jordan taken about 2 years apart showing the dramatic transformation.

After Jordan was changed overnight I felt a strong desire in my spirit to help other parents do the same thing for their hurting children. I knew the pain of ten years, watching my child fall slowly into the dark side. Through no fault of his own he became increasingly more controlled after having been abused only one time by another boy in our neighborhood. Once the spirits gained entry they caused horrific behaviors that no one could stop. The end of torment finally came when I said a simple but very effective prayer with the authority of Christ.

After Jordan mowed my grass that day he called Burger King to set up an interview for employment. He also asked to get his haircut so he would look good for the interview. He was hired two days later and has received promotion after promotion year after year. He became second in command of his own store and was groomed to become General Manager of his own store! He continued to be promoted, taking over poor performing stores around Fishers, Noblesville and Indianapolis and turning them around to performing well. It has been an amazing story and I am so proud of him and where God is taking him.

Chapter 5

Seeing My First Healing Miracles

A couple of months after my son was delivered I told my mentor that I felt led to start reading some Christian books and asked which ones he could recommend. He said the top book was a very short read called *The Believers Authority* by Kenneth E. Hagin. I told him I had not heard of the book and was very excited to start reading it. He said that it would give me a solid base to receive revelation into my Spirit about my true authority in Jesus Christ. John 14:12-14 NKJV *"12Most assuredly, I say to you, he who believes in Me, the works that I do he will do also; and greater works than these he will do, because I go to My father. 13And whatever you ask in My name, that I will do, that the Father may be glorified in the Son. 14 If you ask anything in My name, I will do it."*

I had read that scripture several times before, but I never truly believed that we could actually do the same things that Christ did because I hadn't experienced it. At least I never believed I could actually do what Christ did. I knew there were some people that operated in healing gifts such as Kathryn Kuhlman, Oral Roberts and Benny Hinn but I had no idea how it worked and never knew of anyone that had been healed but I was very intrigued. What if what Jesus said was actually true? I believed the entire Bible to be true, but until you see a miracle for yourself, before your eyes, you can really have a hard time knowing for sure that your authority in Christ is real. Jesus states in Matthew 21:22 NKJV *"And whatever things you ask in prayer, **believing**, you will receive."*

I purchased the Hagin book and immediately began reading. I was surprised to see that it had sold over 2 million copies at that time and I had never heard of it before....or had I? About 3 weeks after I read through it I was in my basement looking through some books I had that were still in boxes and one particularly thin book caught my eye as it looked oddly familiar. As I bent down to pick it up I was stunned to see that it was *The Believer's Authority* by Kenneth E. Hagin! I opened the cover and saw the inscription that my grandmother Finch had written inside back in 1997 stating "All the great men of God have this book as a part of their library!" Wow – I could not believe that I had the book the entire time and yet I had never read it. The top book that my mentor said I should read was the same book that I had owned for 12 years. I felt so sad that I had not read it before now. I could have learned about my authority and prayed over my son right after his incident and he would have been delivered instantly instead of going through ten years of hell! Then the Lord spoke to me. Because I waited I was able to experience what the enemy does to people when they have traumas like my son and so many others in the world. Now I can relate to many more hurting people in the world and help them become free from all enemy spirits. Had I known about it and prayed for him a week after it happened it would not have been much of a testimony to me or Jordan because it would have been just a short blip on our radar screen. There is something about enduring a tribulation for years that forever changes and shapes our character and resolve in a way that a short trial cannot. God wanted to use my pain for His gain. The Lord also told me that all Christians have the ability to command spirits just as Jesus taught, but only if they are aware and have revelation in their spirit. God said he wanted me to teach as many who would listen, how they may live victoriously and not lead fearful or sick lives.

What I learned from Kenneth Hagin is that all believers are given the same authority as Jesus Christ to do the same healing miracles as he did (and commanding other situations in our life beyond just healings) but only if we truly understand and know our authority. Kenneth was born with a deformed heart and an incurable blood disease that no one in the world had survived past the age of fifteen. All that visited him including pastors told him that there was nothing he could do about it and would have to die....but he did not want to die. He heard from the Lord who told him he did not have to depart this life, but he needed to read the Bible to see how. He began to read and was healed supernaturally by the Lord. Later when he became a pastor the Lord gave him more revelation to understand and teach that all believers could live healthy lives but only if they learned of their authority in Christ. So Kenneth was directed to read the book of Ephesians over and over again until he received the revelation in His spirit.

Ephesians 1:18-23 NKJV reads *"[18] the eyes of your understanding being enlightened; that you may know what is the hope of His calling, what are the riches of the glory of His inheritance in the saints, [19] and what is the exceeding greatness of His power toward us who believe, according to the working of His mighty power [20] which He worked in Christ when He raised Him from the dead and seated Him at His right hand in the heavenly places, [21] far above all principality and power and might and dominion, and every name that is named, not only in this age but also in that which is to come. [22] And He put all things under His feet and gave Him to be head over all things to the church, [23] which is His body, the fullness of Him who fills all in all."*

Paul was saying in these verses we the church are the body of Christ and He is the head. If all things are under His feet then all things are under our feet as well but only if we walk in the knowledge of Christ that we too have been given the same power and authority as Christ.

Then in Ephesians 2:4-7 NKJV *"⁴ But God, who is rich in mercy, because of His great love with which He loved us, ⁵ even when we were dead in trespasses, made us alive together with Christ (by grace you have been saved), ⁶ and raised us up together, and made us sit together in the heavenly places in Christ Jesus, ⁷ that in the ages to come He might show the exceeding riches of His grace in His kindness toward us in Christ Jesus."*

We as believers are raised up together with Christ, therefore when we realize that Christ is in us then we are able to perform the same miracles that He did, but only if we truly understand in our spirit and know that we have the same power and authority as Christ. If not then we cannot and will not be able to see miracles and will live defeated and sick lives on earth instead of enjoying God's health all of our days. It is a revelation that you need to have in your spirit. Many in church today have no clue because their pastors do not know or believe and never teach about authority in Christ. The sick and diseased say they are waiting on the Lord and believe they **may** be healed. They lack understanding that they already have been granted the same authority as Christ. Most Christians live a defeated life while the enemy wins by convincing them to believe they cannot command sickness and disease away. They may talk like they know their authority but when the rubber meets the road and they get tested by the enemy with pain or an infirmity their only recourse is to run to the doctors to try to obtain their healing. I know because I used to do that when I did not know my authority. If you do not know your authority you better go to the doctor as well because that is likely your only hope for healing.

After I read *The Believers Authority* several times I was tested by the enemy for the first time to see if I really believed what I had read. One night I was out for a walk in my neighborhood in Noblesville and I started to feel a little pain in one of my teeth. At 10:00 pm the pain level felt like a 4 out of 10 so I went to sleep hoping that the pain would go away after I slept. Instead I woke up around 1:30 am and the pain in my tooth was a 10 out of 10. It was horrible in every way so I went to the kitchen for some ice to put between my teeth hoping the pain would subside. It did not. I wanted to drive myself to the dentist right then it hurt so much, but since it was almost two o'clock on a Sunday morning I knew I was out of luck. Then the Lord spoke to me saying "Use your authority!" I responded "That will never work" in which He replied "What choice do you have? You are in extreme pain and it is two o'clock on a Sunday morning – no dentist is awake and the emergency room at the hospital cannot do anything for you." I admitted He had a good point! Since no one in the house was awake to hear my prayer I decided to give it a shot. So I said out loud with as much authority as I could muster "I command you spirit of infirmity to go NOW in Jesus' name!!" Instantly my pain disappeared! I could not fathom what had just happened. I was stunned in amazement. I opened and shut my mouth with my teeth biting up and down and I felt absolutely no pain whatsoever. Was I dreaming? I smacked my mouth with my hand to make sure and had no pain at all. I shouted out "Oh my gosh!!!" and immediately ran upstairs and woke my wife proclaiming "It works! It works! It works!!!" From that day forward my life was forever changed. This was the greatest revelation that I had ever experienced in my life. I could not believe that more pastors and Christians did not know about this "best kept secret ever!" How could people not know this amazing power that Christ gave to us? Why were churches and pastors not telling people about this everywhere? Next to salvation, it was God's greatest gift to the world!

I remember thinking to myself – what good is it to be saved if we must suffer with the same pain and sickness as an unbeliever? Why would this not be talked about in every church in the world? How is it we hear about amazing miracles in Africa, South America, and many other places around the world but not in the United States or Europe? What do they know that we are not being told or taught by the church? I knew right then and there I would make sure everyone I talked with would hear of this amazing power! I would tell everyone around the world if the Lord would put me on a platform to be heard. I was a financial services software business executive and not a pastor. I learned an amazing principle by hearing from the Lord directly and it changed my life forever. I would never give up until I had convinced every one that I met of the truth of what I had just experienced.

A few months after I witnessed this first miracle I needed another much larger one – much more than just a healed toothache. It happened on a Friday night at my home in Noblesville and I was alone. My son Jordan's girlfriend wanted to give away two puppies and he gladly took them in and gave them to me. I was not pleased because I knew who would be taking care of them. We had them for a couple of weeks and kept them in our kitchen with a makeshift kennel area that consisted of some plastic gates that we connected together in a circle that was about 3 feet high. I reached over the gate to lift a puppy at an awkward angle for my back and all of a sudden I heard a loud "pop." One of my discs in my back had herniated. I walked carefully to the couch and laid down hoping that the expected pain would be minimal. Within minutes I could feel pain envelop my entire body from head to toe. I laid there by myself thinking "I am going to need surgery, back pain never leaves, backs usually gets worse, and what am I going to do!" I allowed myself to get into fear and was definitely not as strong in my faith as I thought I was (most people believe they have faith until truly tested with a lot of pain or a bad report from the lab or doctor). Fear is the opposite of faith!

My wife walked in and asked what I was doing so I told her what just happened. She called our mentor in California and asked him to pray. He started laughing and said "I am not going to pray for Nelson – he is too anointed. It would be like Reinhard Bonnke calling Benny Hinn asking him to pray for his back." He said it was crazy to have him pray for me and that I simply needed to take my authority in Christ and command the healing to occur and pain to go. I was shocked and dismayed that he would not pray one word for me and assured him that I was not too anointed! I was in ridiculous pain that on a scale of 1-10 felt like 100 all over my body. He reiterated that he would not pray for me and I absolutely needed to learn my authority as a believer. He said someday I would be teaching hundreds of thousands of others about their authority in Christ and I needed to learn all about it now. So I lay on the couch in pain all evening holding back the tears. I thought about it for a little while and the Lord told me He would heal me but could only if I stayed in faith. He said that He would always heal me from whatever I had to deal with but not if I allowed myself to slip into fear. He said once I became fearful I was on the enemy's territory. Just as turning on a light causes darkness to leave; having faith will cause fear to leave. Healing cannot happen in an atmosphere of fear. In fear I could only be helped if I went to a doctor to take medications, surgery, and shots, and then hope for the best, etc. I decided right then and there not to take any painkillers but instead take God at His word to see if my faith in Christ's authority would heal me completely. I did not want to get in the way of what God could do by circumventing His ability to supernaturally heal me. So I v-e-r-y s-l-o-w-l-y and painfully crawled upstairs to bed and laid down in excruciating pain. I would put my faith to the test tomorrow. I could not fall asleep much at all and was in pain just lying in bed all night but I wanted to prove to myself that the Bible was true. Either we were given the right to health by Jesus Christ when he died on the cross or we were not.

The next morning I received my biggest test yet from the enemy. Did I believe God would heal me or would I give up and go the ways of man and medicine? I chose God. I began reading *The Believers Authority* once again as well as another faith and miracles book by Jerry Savelle. I gathered the strength to test if I could be healed of this huge mountain of pain by God or not. In my mind I wanted to prove whether what Jesus did and said was real or not. I said to myself that it was time for the truth to come out – either I believed what Paul said in 1 Peter 2:24 NKJV *"who Himself bore our sins in His own body on the tree, that we, having died to sins, might live for righteousness – by whose stripes you were healed."* or I did not. I believed it and wanted to see it work again for me.

I commanded my back to be healed and for pain to leave. I felt no improvement at all so I decided to get out of bed very slowly, stand up, and take some literal steps of faith with 100% pain throughout my body. While my wife watched I very painfully stood up and started to take some baby steps around my bed in the most extreme pain I had ever felt – and speaking out the entire time "I feel great – I am healed – all pain is gone - in Jesus name!" and after walking around the perimeter of the bed for about 5 minutes I laid back in bed very slowly and was still in extreme pain. I could have given up right there because I saw no improvement whatsoever. I could have asked for some painkillers and set an immediate appointment with the doctor. No one would have blamed me – but I would have felt I personally gave up on God. I desperately wanted to believe that He would heal me supernaturally and completely.

So what did I do next? I decided to feed my faith and reread *The Believers Authority* book and more passages in the Bible about healing and God's promises and I decided to take more steps of faith. I very slowly and painstakingly moved my legs from the bed to the floor again and in extreme pain stood up and started to very slowly walk in excruciating pain around my bed speaking out loudly "I am healed...I feel great...All pain is gone...in Jesus name!" gritting my teeth the whole time. Well very slowly by the end of that day my pain level had dropped to 50% of what it was at the start of the day. I was so excited because now I knew I had it beat and that I was going to be completely healed. I knew that I knew that the enemy knew that the pain had to go! I believed that I would be totally healed without a shadow of a doubt the next day. So I went to sleep that night in half as much pain as the previous night and knew in my spirit that the next day I would receive the rest of my healing.

The next day I awoke and still had half the pain but I knew it was just a matter of time before all pain was going to be gone. I continued to speak out "Thank you Jesus I am healed" and little by little my pain continued to lessen and by the end of day two I was 90% better. Thank you Jesus! So I proclaimed from my mouth what I wanted to manifest in the physical. The very next day I awoke to no pain! I decided to get my running shoes on and go for a 3 mile run around the neighborhood. I was just shaking my head in amazement as I was running and had no pain whatsoever – all without taking any painkillers and all by speaking out in faith that I was healed. Praise God!!! I think back to those days and was so very grateful that I passed a test from the enemy who had tried to cause me to fail.

Had I given up and taken Tylenol or ibuprofen and went to the doctor I would have never seen the miracle healing and who knows if I would have ever believed that God would have healed me of anything else later in my life. I would probably not have been able to pray and believe that others would be healed. I was ready for the challenge and I had persevered and trusted God and believed that I would be healed even though my entire body was in the worst pain I had ever felt in my life. Some of you reading this may think that I was unwise and should have gone to the doctor but think about this – had I done just that would I have been seeing all the amazing miracles that I am seeing today and would I have ever written this book on healing? I emphatically would have to say no!

It takes testing by fire to truly separate the men from the boys when it comes to faith in Jesus for healing. The enemy will put up smoke screens and roadblocks in your life and many will not believe, become fearful and give up. It's then and there that you have given away your authority and the enemy wins. You will have to go to the doctor at that point because Jesus cannot heal you. Just like David in 1 Samuel 17 – he could have been like all the other men of Israel who were scared of being killed by Goliath and did not believe that God would give him victory over their mountain. David believed God would deliver his enemy to him – a mere teenager with no armor protection versus an almost 10 foot tall giant with armor all around him who had killed hundreds in his life – yet David was not fearful – he stood in faith and believed He would defeat the giant and 'move that mountain' for him.

Every person's test from the enemy is a little different – for those just starting out in their faith journey it may be something like a doctor telling you that you will always have bronchitis and pneumonia the rest of your life if you ever run outside during the fall or winter months so you stop doing it in fear that you will get sick – but for those with greater faith it may be that you were just diagnosed with 4th stage lung cancer and that you supposedly have only six months to live. Are you going to believe what you have been told or see – or are you going to believe that God will do what He says in the Bible?

Speaking of bronchitis and pneumonia – my next test was one that I brought on myself. Ever since I had caught pneumonia in southern California in the late 1990's and almost died I was worried about what the doctor had told me, that I would have a predisposition to getting bronchitis the rest of my life. Guess what? I always used to get bronchitis and occasionally pneumonia every year after that! If I caught it early enough I would take Zithromax® pills – if not then I would have to take some huge penicillin pills. I decided the winter of 2011-12 to go running outside the entire winter and breathe in as much cold air into my lungs as possible to prove that I would no longer get it as I now knew my authority in Christ to withstand sickness and not live in fear. The first week I ran outside I felt no symptoms whatsoever and it was definitely testing my faith because I knew in the past that I would catch bronchitis very easily. I did not become fearful at all and one week expanded to become one month and then the 2nd month and then into December, January and February, nothing! I caught no bronchitis and just had a minor cold for a couple days before it went away without taking any over the counter meds or other drugs. I conquered my mountain of bronchitis and I have never been afflicted since! What changed? Did my lungs somehow build up immunity to bronchitis? Absolutely not. My mindset changed and as I learned I had the same spirit as Jesus Christ I would no longer catch it. If He would not take bronchitis then neither would I. I knew that I knew that I knew that I would not get it anymore, ever. It was personally such an awesome breakthrough for me to have.

It takes time to build up your faith and little victories over small mountains turn into bigger victories over bigger mountains. I could not have had this breakthrough over bronchitis right after my toothache healing happened – it is a process of bigger and bigger victories over time to allow a person to be tested by what fears and mountains are in their own lives. What is your mountain? Is it diabetes, high blood pressure, ADHD, a leg that is shorter than the other, fear and anxiety, scoliosis, a broken bone or cancer? I strongly encourage you to learn your authority now because it can be a life and death situation later. Learn it now, if not for you, for someone you know. Without authority their lives could be taken from them. That is why it is important to learn about this prior to being in a battle for your life because once you are in fear you have no chance of defeating the enemy and must hope that man's medicine is enough to cure and save you. What kind of faith do you want to have?

The Lord told me I needed to make everyone aware of their authority in Christ because if they are healed by prayer on one night they could lose it the next when the enemy brings a symptom back to them and they are unable to stand against it with their faith to know it is just a symptom until they get into fear and then it can stay on them. Pastors need to understand this for themselves and receive the revelation so they can teach it to the members of their church. What good is it if the pastor is suffering from some physical affliction all the time and how can they tell their congregations to have faith that God will heal them of pain or sickness? Instead they try to explain it away by saying "Well it is up to God whether He heals you or not – so if it is not His will then I guess he must want you to be sick and die." I'm sure this has been repeated numerous times though maybe not exactly in those words! Learn your authority and then walk in it every day and then teach it so others can walk in it too. This revelation will change your life and set you on fire for God all the days of your life! Every church in America should have people coming forward at the end of the service to have people that know their authority command pain and sickness off of their members. There should always be expectancy that they will be healed instantly.

At the end of 2012 I was excited about watching some good college football bowl games because it is one of my most enjoyable times of the year sports-wise, but the Lord was adamant that I officially launch my new ministry. He told me to call it *Restored To Freedom* but I was certain that some company or ministry somewhere in the world had already registered the domain for www.restoredtofreedom.com or org. To my shock no one in the world had either, so I took both. It was confirmation that the Lord wanted me to have both and that the ministry focus would be about helping people who had been severely hurt by the enemy through the actions of others and had physical pain. People would be restored from all emotional pain as well as physical infirmities. Some need

59

deliverance from demonic control and emotional healing as well as from physical afflictions and they would indeed be restored to freedom in Christ. It was most appropriately named by the Lord indeed. Praise God!

Chapter 6

Becoming Stronger in the Lord

In 2013 I began to receive more confidence in my authority to step out and pray for other people and began to see healings in others' lives. Interestingly, I saw many that I prayed for healed from scoliosis and back pain at a very high success rate which was an issue I had to personally overcome in my own life.

One day my wife got a call from a lady who lived somewhere in Indianapolis and said she felt led to call because she had found my ministry website www.restoredtofreedom.com. The woman said she could physically see demons in her home and they would get on top of her in bed and grab her arms and dig their claws into her forearms and also harass and scare her seven year old daughter. I was very excited to take on some demons because I felt I was getting stronger in my authority and was finally up to some real challenges. My wife was not as excited so I ended up talking to the woman over the phone. The woman put me on speaker phone and I listened to the Lord and He told me exactly what to say to command the demons to be gone from her home in Jesus name and she saw and felt them all leave instantly. I listened again to the Lord and He told me demons were there because her mother that lives with her needed to get her life right with the Lord or else they could bring more demons back with them than before. So she talked to her mother and she gave her life to the Lord and they never had an issue with them returning again. It was a great learning experience for me concerning the authority because I would later start praying for more people over the phone and seeing amazing results of victory over sickness and demons.

On my birthday January 2, 2014 I asked the Lord to give me a special word just for me as to what He wanted me to know. He told me once again that He would heal me from everything the rest of my life as long as I did not get into fear. He also added that He wanted me to go on a 21 day fast of only drinking water. Up to that point I had only fasted a few times in my life because I really liked eating. I fasted for 3 days when I was a senior at Purdue and felt like I was going to die I was so hungry and weak by the third day. I remember taking an exam in my Supervision class believing I failed it because I could not remember anything from studying on an empty stomach but I actually received an A along with very few other students in the class. The last time I had fasted was for a week in August of 2013 and I only drank water then as well. I felt very weak the last couple days of that fast but made it through. I was up to the 21 day challenge and during the entire process learned much I was not aware of which matured me spiritually.

During the first few days of the fast I decided to study from a non-Christian perspective the benefits of a water-only fast. I was amazed at what I found on the internet. Many sites talked about how the body would go into a self-preservation mode and start going after various sicknesses and diseases and actually heal the body. I learned that our body uses as the primary source of energy a sugar called glucose, most of it coming from the food we eat. The glucose in excess is then stored in the liver and transformed in a reserve of glycogen. When we fast, the same healing process that happens during our sleep takes place. The glycogen is then used to recover damaged tissues and, when finished, the body shifts over to ketosis, using fats as the main source of energy. Usually the ketosis process starts after the first three days of fasting and, after seven days, the body, in order to preserve its protein (muscle), starts turning nonessential cellular masses such as fibroid tumors and degenerative tissues, bacteria, viruses, or any other compounds in the body into energy. Consequently, the body starts healing itself from all kinds of diseases and infirmities! Perhaps this is why the Bible mentions fasting almost as many times as praying!

I learned that detoxification is a normal body process of eliminating or neutralizing toxins through the colon, liver, kidneys, lungs, lymph glands, and skin. During water fasting, all the toxins in our body are expelled, creating inside the body an ideal environment for healthy growth. This is responsible for healthier skin, teeth and gums. Amazing!

Some of the most common diseases reported to have been healed through fasting of 21 or more days drinking only water are: high blood pressure, asthma, allergies, chronic headaches, inflammatory bowel disease (ulcerative colitis and Crohn's disease), irritable bowel syndrome, adult onset diabetes, heart disease, degenerative arthritis, rheumatoid arthritis, psoriasis, eczema, acne, uterine fibroids, benign tumors, and systemic lupus erythematosus. You may also experience better sleep, more energy and of course loss of excess weight. This really amazed me but also made an impact on me because I now realized why it was so important to take periodic fasts so that the body would heal itself naturally. If you think about how many people today are overweight and eat foods that are high in fat, fried, high in sugar and salt – it is no wonder so many are living a life full of sickness and premature death. Their bodies simply cannot get a break in order to repair themselves.

When I started my 21 day water only fast I knew that I needed to lose a few pounds as it was right after the holidays and I had gained

8-10 more pounds than I normally felt comfortable weighing. I also reviewed information on the internet from various Christians like Jentezen Franklin and Bill Bright (who once did annual 40 day water only fasts) and others on the spiritual benefits from fasting and learned:

• It is a biblical way to truly humble oneself in the sight of God (Psalms 35:13 NKJV - *But as for me, when they were sick, My clothing was sackcloth; I humbled myself with fasting; And my prayer would return to my own heart.";* Ezra 8:21 - *Then I proclaimed a fast there at the river of A-hava, that we might humble ourselves before our God, to seek from Him the right way for us and our little ones and all our possessions.)*
• It brings revelation by the Holy Spirit of a person's true spiritual condition, resulting in brokenness, repentance and change.
• It is a crucial means for personal revival because it brings the inner workings of the Holy Spirit into play in a most unusual and powerful way.
• It helps us better understand the word of God by making it more meaningful, vital and practical.
• It transforms prayer into a richer and more personal experience.
• It increases the power in one's life to see more authority over the enemy when commanding spirits that are afflicting someone.

The Lord told me to read Matthew 17:14-21 NKJV *"[14] And when they had come to the multitude, a man came to Him, kneeling down to Him and saying, [15] 'Lord, have mercy on my son, for he is an epileptic and suffers severely; for he often falls into the fire and often into the water. [16] So I brought him to Your disciples, but they could not cure him'. [17] Then Jesus answered and said, 'O faithless and perverse generation, how long shall I be with you? How long shall I bear with you? Bring him here to Me.' [18] And Jesus rebuked the demon, and it came out of him; and the child was cured from that very hour. [19] Then the disciples came to Jesus privately and said, 'Why could we not cast it out?' [20] So Jesus said to them, "Because of your unbelief, for assuredly, I say to you, if you have faith as a mustard seed, you will say to this mountain, 'Move from here to there' and it will move; and nothing will be impossible for you. [21] However, this kind does not go out except by prayer and fasting."*

So the Lord was telling me that in order to cast out certain strong evil spirits from people that I would need to do a longer fast than just a few days or a week. Thus doing a 21 day or longer water only fast would help me to gain strength over them. The pastor that married me and my wife, Owen Mason from Lafayette, had told me that he also had completed a 21 day water only fast and it was by far the hardest thing that he had ever done and he almost gave up after day 16. It is interesting when you keep food from your body that long, how much you actually think about food throughout the day. It seemed to constantly be on my mind and it was extremely hard when you drive past restaurants and can smell the food cooking.

So I began my task and was looking forward to it wholeheartedly as I wanted to get stronger in the spirit and tell my flesh what to do and break through into a higher level of authority. I really wanted to be able to command any spirit to be gone from any person in the world.

Galatians 5:16-26 NKJV "*16 I say then: Walk in the Spirit, and you shall not fulfill the lust of the flesh. 17 For the flesh lusts against the Spirit, and the Spirit against the flesh; and these are contrary to one another, so that you do not do the things that you wish. 18 But if you are led by the Spirit, you are not under the law. 19 Now the works of the flesh are evident, which are: adultery, fornication, uncleanness, lewdness, 20 idolatry, sorcery, hatred, contentions, jealousies, outbursts of wrath, selfish ambitions, dissensions, heresies, 21 envy, murders, drunkenness, revelries, and the like; of which I tell you beforehand, just as I also told you in time past, that those who practice such things will not inherit the kingdom of God. 22 But the fruit of the Spirit is love, joy, peace, longsuffering, kindness, goodness, faithfulness, 23 gentleness, self-control. Against such there is no law. 24 And those who are Christ's have crucified the flesh with its passions and desires. 25 If we live in the Spirit, let us also walk in the Spirit. 26 Let us not become conceited, provoking one another, envying one another.*"*

I will say this – many men (and women) may want to act like they are extremely powerful in the Lord and may be able to pray prayers that sound very strong and impressive – but a 21 day water only fast will definitely prove out who is all talk and who is truly strong in the Spirit. I have met many people who can act like they are the most spiritual people in the world but when it comes down to denying their flesh food for a few days you will quickly separate the men from the boys. I personally know of two men that did 40 day water only fasts and I have the utmost respect for both of them. I believe that someday the Lord will call me to do a 40 day water fast but until then I will wait patiently. Talk with your mentor or pastor and see how many days they have denied themselves anything but water and you will see who they really are in Christ. Moses, Elijah and Jesus all did 40 day fasts with no food. There is truly something that happens in a man when he denies himself all food and drinks just water for 21 or more days.

Since I had already completed a seven day water only fast a few months prior I knew that I would have no issue with the first week. Also for those of you that may have questions about what goes on with your body – usually after about the third day you no longer excrete waste as your body no longer has food stored up to eliminate which is a benefit to the whole process of purging toxins.

I enjoyed reading the Bible and drawing closer to the Lord during the first week. During the 2nd week there were times that if I stood up too quickly I could have fainted as I was not used to fasting more than a week. There was one time that I did stand up too fast to walk to the bathroom from my bedroom and I actually fainted falling to the floor and slightly bruising myself. I came back to consciousness immediately and recovered quickly as I drank some water. Fortunately my wife was on the phone in our bedroom and did not know that I fell or she would have tried to get me to stop as she was fearful of me doing it for 21 days. I will say that drinking only water for 21 days caused me to lose my enjoyment for the taste of water as it became somewhat repulsive to me. I looked forward every day to brushing my teeth so that I had a little taste on my taste buds but never allowed myself to swallow any of it. I started to develop a rash on my stomach and inside of my arms around day 15 and it lasted until after I had gone off my fast. Fortunately I had read that a rash was possible as the toxins left my body so I was not shocked and did not ever get in fear. My tongue became whiter and pastier and if I ever stood up too fast I could become very light headed, dizzy and might easily faint. It was an amazing experience for me and one that I will forever treasure even though it was the hardest thing that I have ever done to this point in my life.

During my fast I was teaching ten men every Thursday evening in my Westfield home about *The Believers Authority* and as a part of that I would purchase Papa John's pizza and a giant cookie for everyone. After you have not eaten for several weeks the aroma of Papa John's pizza in your car is tantamount to being tortured. It was extremely tempting to not cheat and eat just a tiny piece but I knew I could not because God would know, as well as the demons! One thing that I had never thought about before I did the fast was that I was really missing the feeling of actually chewing food and after 3 weeks of not chewing it is a great feeling to resume eating again (be sure when you resume food to start small and mild in the beginning. Broth and cooked vegetables are best).

I could feel my body getting weaker yet my spirit felt stronger and the Lord told me that I was gaining more authority in the spirit realm against demons and it would be used later in my ministry. After 21 days were up I could not wait to eat and had to ease slowly back into feeding my flesh again. I had wanted to be set free from eating processed sugar and indeed I was as fruit was my new sugar that I desired. No more cookies or desserts. I had lost 30 lbs during the 3 weeks and went from 183 to 153 pounds which was seven pounds under my high school graduation weight. I felt great afterward and could hear the Lord's voice even clearer as He was telling me I still had many things to overcome in the future. I was now more than ever in my life equipped to handle all the enemy would do to come against me.

In March of 2014 I attended my first Power and Love School (PowerAndLove.org) near St. Louis where Todd White was speaking, a man the Lord told me I should meet. For those of you that have never heard of Todd let me try to explain him to you. He is unlike anyone you will ever meet as he is the real, authentic and genuine deal – someone that I had the utmost respect for while watching his many street healing videos on the internet and seeing him interviewed on the Sid Roth show. Todd's parents were divorced when he was young and one summer his mother put him in a Masonic home and was to pick him up at the end of summer but instead left him there for several years. When Todd came out of the home he was a very angry young man who had lost all of his faith and became an atheist. He soon became a drug dealer and one night was dealing and pretended to be a policeman in order to get free drugs and started to read the person his rights. Then he took off in his vehicle but the guy pulled out a gun and shot about five times from a short distance as he drove his vehicle away. None of the bullets penetrated his vehicle and he heard the Lord for the first time speak to him saying "I took those bullets for you, are you ready to serve Me?" Eventually he became a Christian and had a desire to truly love on hurting people. It took him praying for about 700 people before he started seeing healings but now he ministers at a very high level, healing people through Christ and teaching others to do the same. Personally I think I would have given up after the first ten people if I had not seen anyone healed that I prayed for so this was amazing faith and perseverance on Todd's part. It was such an honor to be able to meet him for the first time. I went to shake his hand to thank him for flying all the way from Hawaii (a close friend of his lost his son in an auto accident so he flew from Philadelphia to Hawaii before coming back to St. Louis) and instead of shaking my hand he said "No dude – I hug" and gave me a great big hug!! He was awesome. He wears long dreadlocks and has a great singing voice and had only been a Christian for 10 years. I felt the Lord was telling me I would soon be doing street ministry and more just like Todd but I could hardly imagine I would have the faith to do what he did.

On Father's Day in 2014 I went swimming at a water park in Plainfield, Indiana and my 19 year old daughter Ashley, stepson and wife noticed a small bulge in the middle of my back on my spine. I could feel it when I touched it but did not get into fear as I now knew my authority. I never spoke to it though nor commanded it to go so around August the bulge started to grow rapidly. It grew to the size of a golf ball and I would not take my shirt off anymore and did not show it to my wife because she did not have the same level of faith for healing I had and would have recommended I see a doctor. I commanded the growth to go but it did not dissolve. A week had passed and when I slept on it I felt pain in my back and also when I drove I felt pain. My stepson hugged me once and could feel the bulge and was grossed out (which made me feel sorry I allowed him to hug me). I did not get into fear though and knew it had to go because I knew my authority in Christ and that this was just a lame attempt by the enemy to see if I would flinch and get into fear. After the second week I continued to thank the Lord that it was gone but it still did not dissolve. After the third week it was as big as ever and as painful as ever and it literally felt like I was sleeping on a golf ball! By the fourth week I was becoming really annoyed it had not dissolved and to top things off my wife started complaining that she was having vision problems of blurriness and talked about going to the doctor. I finally had enough of what was happening and asked the Lord what was going on because we had always been healed of every infirmity for the previous 5+ years. He told me that He wanted my wife to be in unity of spirit with me especially in the area of physical healing and later there would be a similar physical infirmity that she would have to overcome so He wanted her to pray for me and I would pray for her and the problems would be resolved.

At last, I took off my shirt and showed her my back for the first time. She was shocked and thought I needed to go to the doctor (which I knew she would say) so I told her to stop talking fear and just command the bulge to go and I would pray for her vision to be healed and our problems would be solved. So she prayed for me and I prayed for her. From that day forward she no longer had any vision problems. But the bulge in my back remained just as big and painful as ever. So I went to bed in full faith knowing that it would dissolve away. I did not get into fear because I knew it was already gone in the spirit since the prayer was spoken and now I just needed to wait in peace until the bulge manifested in the physical and shrank, so I thanked God for healing me. The next day came and it was yet the same size and as painful as ever. I refused to get into fear because I knew that I knew it was going to go. Finally on the third day I noticed that it had become just a tiny bit smaller, maybe five percent, then I knew it was finally going to go. Little by little every day it began to shrink and by the end of the third week it was completely gone. Some have asked me 'what was it?' I respond with 'I don't know' since I never went to the doctor, silly. I suspect it could have been a cyst or a tumor but it really did not matter to me. In my mind I knew whatever it was had to go because of my faith. So my question to the reader is - where is your faith? If you had a golf ball sized bulge appear on your back that lasted 7 weeks would you stay in faith the whole time or would you become fearful for five minutes or days or weeks? From my personal experience when I have stayed in faith the Lord has healed me every single time. Every time from everything! Yes my faith is extremely strong now but seven years ago when I first started learning about my authority there would have been no way I would have been able to be free from fear with a painful bulge in my back, but that is how faith works. As you grow in it you are able to withstand more significant circumstances without becoming fearful. The enemy wanted to scare me but he could not and now I am extremely strong in the Lord. I know that the enemy will never stop – as I will continue to have even larger mountains to stand up to; perhaps not physical but definitely circumstantial.

When I see people get into fear concerning physical afflictions I tell them they have to go to the doctor because you are no longer in faith and you are on enemy territory so you must go to the doctor. I believe that the Lord waited so long to heal me for several reasons –

> 1) To help me learn that no matter how long something is on me, as long as I stay in faith and not fear He would heal me.
> 2) To help my wife see that if she would ever encounter an infirmity, He would heal her as long as she did not get in fear (interestingly she ended up getting a cyst just a few months later).
> 3) To allow other people to hear my testimony in order to encourage them that as long as they stayed in faith and did not allow fear to enter in then He would do the same for them.

Hear me clearly on this – faith for healing is not for the weak of heart. If you do not have the faith to believe you will be healed then you need to go to the doctor because you will not be able to be healed. Faith and fear are opposite. Does God want to heal all His people? Absolutely yes. Can He heal you if you are afraid and in fear? Usually not. Although if you are a non-believer I have seen people get healed much more consistently because the Lord wants to draw them to Him which healings do all the time.

This is what I have seen play out because our lack of faith will stop what God can do. Think about the Israelites in Numbers – Caleb and Joshua believed they could overtake the giants in the Promised Land of Canaan but the other ten spies were afraid and said no. Because the Israelites were in fear, based upon the word of ten spies, they could not cross into the Promised Land and had to wander in the desert for forty years until all the faithless people had died. Faith is an individual position and not to be taken lightly. If you want to compete against your spouse on faith (which I would not recommend) you are on dangerous ground. Do not say that you have as much faith as your spouse if you know you do not because faith is not a competition and sooner or later you will be tested and fail. Yes, God would want all His people to have faith like Abraham, but it takes time, it takes overcoming tests from the enemy, it takes humbleness, and it also requires fasting and denying your flesh to get stronger in the Lord. Above all it is an individual mindset you cannot acquire from your spouse. Please do not berate your spouse if they have a stronger faith than you. Also, do not denigrate a spouse that has the weaker faith. You who are stronger should never flaunt your faith or diminish your spouse that has less – if you do then the Lord will correct you and it is never fun to be corrected by Him. Recognize where each of you are and continue to help each other grow in faith so that the enemy will never have the upper hand on either of you or the marriage.

Joyce Meyer talks about a woman that was attending Bible studies in her home and would get really sick from being pregnant and could not attend the morning studies. Joyce would verbally make fun of her because Joyce had never had morning sickness with any of her babies. The very next time Joyce was pregnant, guess what? She was sick the entire pregnancy. Why? Joyce said the Lord wanted her to learn not to be so judgmental of someone else. So make sure you never put down anyone who does not have the same faith as you. Instead, be loving and gentle and pray for them to come up to your level.

In 2014 I was serving at a church in Fishers, Indiana in the Healing Rooms but something inside of me said that I really wanted to do more than just heal a couple of times a month. It was good initial training to be able to see some people and practice but my heart was to pray for many more and on a more frequent basis. While serving there I had prayed for several men with severe back injuries (slipped discs, bulging discs) and they were instantly healed. Also there was an Egyptian man who had broken his foot playing soccer 2 weeks before (and had walked in on crutches). After prayer he was jumping up and down dancing with no pain. I was reading about the life of the great healer John G. Lake from the early 1900's during this time and I had a vision that I would someday have my own Healing Rooms and see many more miracle healings as well as teach people how they could heal as Jesus did. Everything in my spirit wanted to teach others that they could see the same miracles Jesus did if only they had the faith to believe. My passion was like John G. Lake – I really wanted to have a Healing Room open every day of the week and heal people. I also want to teach people and allow them to come and observe in the rooms to learn and go back to their towns and cities to open their own Healing Rooms.

The week before Thanksgiving 2014 a church in Fishers took a team of their Healing Room trained volunteers to a church in Elkhart, Indiana that had people from a white and black church that were coming together and we were to do a night of healing. Prior to us going to the church on a Wednesday night the Lord told me to go on another seven day water only fast. On the first day of the fast (Monday) at lunch time the Lord spoke to me and told me all of the healings that were going to take place (backs, necks, stroke, hemorrhoids, broken bones, hearts, arthritis, etc) about 15 in all. So I read the list of infirmities that the Lord told me were going to see healed to the leader who was driving us to Elkhart prior to when our team left the church. Then on the drive to the Elkhart church the Lord spoke to him and told him to have me read my list and that every item I read, someone would stand up who had that very infirmity. He did not tell me he was going to have me come up and read the list until he was speaking to the entire church and then surprised me in front of everyone that he wanted me to read off the list. As I began reading the first infirmity one person stood up, then the next infirmity 2 more people stood up, one by one there were either one or more persons who had those conditions. It was a very unique way that the Lord was speaking to everyone's faith because only the Lord would know what each of them had and who would be attending so by the time I was done reading the 15 or so infirmities on my list about 90% of the church was standing ready to be healed. We had them all come forward and we began praying and they all were healed. It was a great scene to be part of and observe how the Lord worked. We arrived home in Westfield at 1 am and we all were exhausted but I knew the Lord was going to eventually have me take teams to churches in the future and I was so excited because it gave me a vision of what was about to happen and how much fun it would be for everyone both to give and for those that were receiving.

Chapter 7

Greater Healing and Deliverance

2015 was a year of tremendous personal breakthrough for me as the Lord launched me into the greatest year of my young ministry life. I was free to go anywhere He directed me and wherever I went I saw lives changed as I poured out love on His people. I had received many prophecies from numerous people over the previous six years and they were now finally starting to come to pass. It was a wondrous and beautiful thing for me to witness.

I was able to attend the last night of a 52 day revival that broke out in the Elkhart/Goshen area. I arrived just 20 minutes before it was to start and was told the main parking was full and the main church (which met in a former movie theater) was full and I would need to go to a satellite church miles away. The Lord told me He had a place for me and to continue to drive in. Since I was taking an older friend who was 88 years old I decided to at least let him walk into the main church to see how crowded it was, so I dropped him at the front door. Then, when I drove around the full parking lot I noticed a huge pile of snow about 10 feet tall and noticed a car parked next to it with more than enough room for another car beside it – yay, favor! When I walked in to find my friend, he had already gotten seats and we were both given free food! We were so grateful and thankful for this favor from the Lord.

Later in 2015 we were able to attend other revivals in Indiana: Kokomo, Bloomington, Fort Wayne, South Bend and we hosted revival with a group of pastors in Hamilton County in the town of Westfield. What an awesome year of revival to watch unfold across the state. We were able to meet the man that started the revival, a former Amish man named Dennis Miller who had prayed for many years that revival would break out in the land of Goshen!

In February and March of 2015, I started getting requests to provide Holy Spirit led counsel to men and women from around central Indiana and I was paid for the first time in my life for ministry. I was so grateful to the Lord for finally receiving some financial remuneration for doing what I had wanted to do since my son was delivered in 2009. It was such a blessing to provide words from the Lord to people that needed to have some guidance and help with emotional healing and a greater peace in their lives.

In April I attended another Power and Love School with Todd White and another awesome man named Robby Dawkins whom I had yet to meet in person. I took my good friends Bob Mann and Nova Christie and I told them their lives would be changed forever by attending the 3 day conference near Dayton, Ohio. Little did I know my life would also be changed forever for attending the conference with them as God had something planned and did not share with me so I could be surprised. On the first night of the conference Robby Dawkins spoke and it was the first time I had met him in person. Many people came to the front of the sanctuary at the end, me included. Robby specifically came up to me and prayed over me declaring that I would have a double anointing from the Lord. Immediately I felt the presence of the Lord all over me very strongly for about 30 minutes so I knew something very significant was going on.

Robby Dawkins (on the previous page) the night he prayed for me to have a double anointing.

After the conference I drove back to my home in Carmel, arriving early Sunday morning. I was planning to go to New Life Assembly of God in Noblesville, but when I woke up the Lord told me He wanted me to attend Church Alive in Lafayette, Indiana. I wrestled with the decision and with the Lord because I really did not feel like driving an hour to Lafayette, especially when Pastor Owen Mason did not know I was coming. I obeyed anyway.

On my drive up to Lafayette the Lord spoke to me to reveal what was about to happen at the church. He said that I was going to be praying over about 1/3 of the church for healing and they would be healed. I said "What – that will never happen!" and He said "Yes, it will" and I said "No, it won't" and He said "Watch and see." So I arrived right before the second service was to start and said hello to Pastor Owen who was surprised to see me. After the worship had concluded he arose to speak and the Lord spoke to me again saying "Get ready – he is going to tell you to come up and pray for people." Again I told God it would not happen. Then Owen said "We have a visitor here today from Indianapolis who has seen a lot of healings in his life so I would like to have Nelson Schuman come up and pray for people today." I was shocked, amazed, humbled and blown away at what God was doing for me. So I started praying for people and saw them getting healed from torn rotator cuffs, Fibro Myalgia, back pain, addictions, etc, and prayed for about 1/3 of the church and it took about 90 minutes. I could not believe what had just happened after it was all over. Then Owen took me out to lunch and afterward gave me a personal check for $100 toward my ministry. I was so grateful and thankful I just cried to the Lord in awe. What had been prophesied over me for the past 6 years by many people from around the world was at last coming to pass. I knew that the Lord's hand was strong upon me as everything in my spirit was so excited and humbled.

My faith skyrocketed after that and I started looking for people to pray for everywhere. At LA Fitness where I worked out, on the streets, malls, work, nursing homes, rehab places, church and more, many were being healed instantly. The success rate of healing literally doubled from about 40-45% to 80-90%. I was so thankful to the Lord for blessing me. All I really wanted to do is what Jesus said we could do and now I was seeing it come to pass.

Also, I started seeing people delivered from the most difficult spirit to become free of called the Jezebel spirit. Many say that it is impossible to be delivered from it but I now had a strong anointing over it due to what I had endured and because of my 21 day water fast. The Jezebel spirit is comprised of spirits of control, manipulation, lying, anger, and other nasty things. It manifests due to an unloving father who often rejects the child and can be very controlling. Also a mother that treats her child harshly and unlovingly can help develop the same spirit. It was astounding to me because the Lord brought people to me week after week who either had the Jezebel spirit, were married to someone who had it, had divorced someone who had it, or knew of someone who had it. I was amazed that so many people kept coming to me and knew it was the Lord showing me that there are a lot of people who have no peace and could not understand why they were unable to have good relationships. After I had them read a prayer the majority were instantly delivered. Some denied they had Jezebel and continued to suffer in their lives from either physical sickness and disease or their relational or financial circumstances worsened. If they finally admitted they had been in agreement with that spirit, and would read the prayer to get rid of it with fervency, they would be delivered and set free.

Many people after having been delivered made comments later that they could honestly say they were not a real Christian before they were set free. Others said they were Christian only by their outward appearance, because Jezebel is a difficult spirit to discern. They knew how they treated their spouses behind closed doors was not Godly whatsoever. Many said they had received some counseling from multiple pastors and trained counselors but none of these professionals had a clue about delivering people from Jezebel and some even denied there is a Jezebel spirit today. Hosea 4:6 NKJV *"My people are destroyed for lack of knowledge."* Ignorance of the truth and how to truly set hurting people free from enemy oppression is extremely grieving to the Holy Spirit. No longer can we put our heads in the sand or look the other way. Instead we need to press in and learn from the Holy Spirit as to what is real and how to help people obtain deliverance. Telling people you love them yet letting them suffer with spirits attacking them is not real love at all. Do what Jesus commanded. Jesus said in Mark 16:17 NKJV *"And these signs will follow those who believe: in My name they will cast out demons; they will speak with new tongues;"* When you know your authority you can cast out demons from people and set them free. With some demons such as the Spirit of Jezebel and Leviathan you need to lead them through prayers of renunciation to get them delivered as they have to want the spirits gone. It is a beautiful and loving process to watch a person become free from a lifetime of torment in Jesus name.

After months of having Divine encounters, the Lord told me to write a document that would help hundreds more receive freedom from the Jezebel spirit instantly and save their marriages. Finally, one Friday evening in June I sat down and within a few hours had written a document to explain to people who suffered from Jezebel, why they developed it and the traits that they would exhibit and the physical afflictions that normally accompanied it along with a prayer of renunciation. Many pastors asked for the document so they could send it to people in their congregations they knew were struggling with multiple divorces and in current strife-filled marriages and relationships. Women become afflicted by Jezebel much more often than men due to their sensitive hearts being hurt by their fathers more easily. You can learn much more about the Jezebel and Leviathan spirits and how they hurt people in order to hurt their spouses and families in my book *Restored To Freedom*.

My pastor Tim Brown of New Life Assembly of God in Noblesville had wanted to open a Healing Room his entire career as a pastor but never had anyone he knew who had his same heart's desire or knew their authority in Christ or had seen a high rate of healings that could serve as the director. He became aware of what God was doing through me and asked in May if I would be willing to start a Healing Room at New Life. I prayed about it but did not feel like the timing was quite right. I did believe that before the end of 2015 the Lord would say to move forward.

Beginning at New Life after every service I began to see more and more people being healed from all kinds of afflictions. One man that was missing a disc in his lower back got healed instantly and had no more pain and could touch his toes. Another man who had scoliosis his whole life had his back straighten up and had one leg shorter than the other and it grew right out and he had no more pain. A mother had a leg shorter than the other so I commanded it to grow out and it did in seconds. She then asked her 15 year old son, whose leg was about an inch shorter than the other and always walked with his head bobbing up and down, to come up front to let me pray for him. Instantly his leg grew out and he was so thankful and grateful to the Lord because now he could walk normally for the first time in his life.

I was invited by my good friend Judy Doty to attend a Christian street event called Walk of Faith in Anderson, Indiana in June and they had a prayer tent. The problem was that people who came to the event did not have expectations of becoming healed when they were near the tent so I had to go out from the tent and find people that looked like they had pain to get them healed. The first one was a boy who had a wrestling injury from the week before and was wearing a sling on his right arm so I was eager to pray for him. I asked him what happened and he said that he tore his ligament so I asked if I could pray and he said yes so I said "Arm be healed pain be gone in Jesus name" and instantly he felt heat and the pain was gone so he threw away his sling and enjoyed the rest of the day. Then I met a woman who was to have knee surgery and I prayed for her and her knees were healed. A woman's five year old son had pain in his legs while walking and the doctors did not know what to do, so I prayed for him and his pain left and he started running. Then I met a man who had over 70 heart surgeries ask me to pray for him and immediately he felt tremendous heat on his heart and was sweating profusely for over ten minutes and felt his heart get healed. More and more people came up and wanted prayer because now they could see people were being healed and their faith level went from being very low to now being expectant. It was a great learning experience for me and reminded me of what Todd White did when he prayed for people on the street.

One day I drove to downtown Indianapolis and met Bob Mann, Gina Kansteiner and Carrie Basso with her four children to pray over the property that was going to be hosting the annual Gay Pride festival. After we were done praying over the property I noticed a man walking on the street in the distance and it was apparent that one of his legs was much shorter than the other. So I ran over to catch up to him as he was walking. I explained to him that I prayed for people and they would be healed. I had noticed one leg was a lot shorter than the other and if he would allow me pray, his leg would grow out. He said he knew his leg was much shorter but it was ok because he had CP. I was not sure what CP stood for so said "That's fine that you have CP, but I really want to pray for you because I know your leg will grow out, I see it happen all the time." After pleading with him a couple of times he reluctantly agreed to let me pray (more to get me off his back than any faith he may have had), so I was thrilled. He sat down on a concrete bench next to Pennsylvania Street and when I lined his legs up his right leg was at least two inches shorter than the left. So I said "Right leg become equal with the left in Jesus name" and instantly the leg starts growing out and in seconds it is the same length as his other. He looks in stunned silence. Yay Jesus!! I then told him to stand up and say "Thank you Jesus for healing my leg" which he repeated and then I told him to go for a walk now and when he did he was able to walk perfectly normal for the first time in 35 years. Yay Jesus! I came back to meet with Carrie, Gina and Bob and asked them if they knew what CP stood for and Bob said "I believe that stands for Cerebral Palsy", and I said "Yay - Jesus just healed a guy's leg who had Cerebral Palsy!"

Back at New Life Assembly of God in Noblesville I continued to see people healed almost every time they came up at the end of service. On Father's Day morning as I was taking a shower the Lord told me that my 20 year old daughter Ashley was going to heal people at the end of service with me. I was shocked that He said this because she had never prayed for anyone to be healed her entire life. So again I questioned God and said "Really?" and He said "Yes." So I met my daughter at church (she drove from Chesterfield) and introduced her to several people, then at the end of the service I went up to pray for people. I said nothing to my daughter about trying to get her to come up with me as I wanted it to be all her and none of my coercing her. I wanted to see God do what He said would happen. Sure enough she walked up from the second pew and stood alongside of me. I was getting ready to pray for an 18 year old girl whose hip kept popping out so I had the girl put her own hand on her hip and then asked Ashley if she would put her hand on the girl's hand which she agreed to do. Then I put my hand on my daughter's hand and said "Hip be healed in Jesus name" and immediately we all felt the hip pop back into place and she had no more clicking when she moved her leg up and down. My daughter was amazed as she could feel the bone popping into place. Then we had an older lady from Anderson visiting who had scoliosis of her spine (curvature) so I told my daughter that she was going to speak to it and command it to be straight. She was unsure at first but I told her to simply say "Spine and discs be aligned straight in Jesus name" and Ashley repeated it and immediately the woman's spine became straight and she grew an inch taller before our eyes. My daughter said she could see her spine move under the woman's blouse and thought it was amazing. Then we checked the length of her legs and her right leg was about an inch shorter so I had my daughter hold her legs and command the leg to grow out. The lady felt her feet moving and then the leg grew out to match as we video recorded it. The lady then stood up and was in balance for the first time in her life and hugged my daughter and thanked her and they both had tears of love and joy in their eyes. I was so thankful to God to see my daughter do her very first healings.

I continued to pray and see more people healed on the streets around Carmel, Noblesville and Fishers and they were being healed everywhere from everything. Also, more people who had the Jezebel and Leviathan spirits kept bumping into me and I was able to make them aware of why their relationships were failing. They read the renunciation prayers and the spirits left them and their marriages were being restored.

On a Wednesday night after church at New Life Assembly a 29 year old woman approached me as I was getting ready to walk out of the church. She said that she had seen a lot of people on my video testimonies at church and many that went to our church whose legs grew out that were shorter than their other legs but she asked if I thought that her foot could grow out to match her other foot. I was very intrigued by her statement as I had never heard of someone having one much shorter foot. She went on to explain that she was born with a club foot and so it was about an inch shorter (more than a full shoe size) than her other foot. So I said "Yes - I want to see God heal that!" so I brought her up to sit in the front pew and her mother watched as I put my hands around the shorter foot and commanded "Foot grow in Jesus name." Immediately I felt tendons, ligaments and bones around the middle of her foot moving and she felt it moving and it began to slowly grow longer. I had no idea how long it was going to take to grow out as I had never seen a foot grow out but it ended up being about five minutes and it was completely the same length as the other foot. I was very impressed with how Jesus did that and her mom was shocked and amazed. Then the girl commented how she had accidentally broken a bone in the top of the foot that just grew out when she hit it on her bed post so I grabbed the foot and said "Bone be healed in Jesus name" and instantly we could feel the bone coming together. Then she said she had an umbilical hernia so I had her put her hand on her stomach and said "umbilical hernia dissolve in Jesus name" and instantly she felt it dissolve. So within about seven minutes she got a foot lengthened, bone healed and umbilical hernia dissolved. Jesus can do amazing things when we have faith to believe!!!

On another Wednesday night after church a girl asked if I could pray for her boyfriend at home who had a painful cyst on his wrist and needed surgery. I said sure and asked what his phone number was. She did not expect me to pray for him on the phone as she just wanted me to pray in general. I told her I never saw any of those prayers work because the person did not have an actual event being tied to Jesus healing them (and I had never seen those prayers ever work for me). So she gave me his number and I called him. I told him I wanted him to put his hand on the cyst and then I would pray and he would feel some heat and the cyst would dissolve in seconds. So he put his hand on his cyst and then I said "Wrist be healed – cyst be gone in Jesus name" and then he told me he was feeling heat on his wrist. I told him that he was being healed and to give it a few more seconds and it should be gone. Then a few seconds later I told him to take his hand off his wrist where the cyst used to be and I heard him gasp loudly over the phone. He said "Oh my gosh it is gone!" I told him to say thank you Jesus for healing me, which he did. Then I saw him at church Sunday morning and he showed me the picture taken previously of the cyst and showed me that it was now gone from his wrist.

A friend of mine invited me to come to St. Vincent's hospital on 86th Street in Indianapolis to pray for a woman who had strong pain in her lower region. She had just come from surgery and was yet in a lot of pain. We prayed over her and immediately she started feeling more pain in the area where she had the surgery. I thought to myself "Hmmm....more pain is not good Jesus – hurry up and make the pain go away" and about two minutes later, she felt the pain begin to lessen and then she started feeling what she described as butterfly feelings way deep down inside of her that felt very good. Then she told us she had a strange disease named Arnold Chiari Malformation which is an issue where the brain seeps through the lower part of the skull and produces a lot of headaches and migraines. So I prayed for that and she felt a strong heat taking away the pain from the back of her neck. She could move her head all around and did not have any more pain or hear any clicking noises. Then she said she could feel Jesus putting his arms around her and comforting her and it was an amazing feeling of love.

Several days later a classmate of mine from high school asked me to drive to Warsaw, Indiana to pray over her because she had many health issues. When I met with her and saw the list of items that she needed healing from, the Lord told me that she first needed to get free from a spirit which attacks people through growing up with fathers that wound their children by unloving and controlling behavior. As I was telling her about it she started to try to read the prayer and she felt something trying to stop her from reading it. She felt her chest was being constricted by something. I told her it was just the spirits on her trying to stop her from commanding them to go. So she started to read the prayer and after a few sentences her voice changed to be more at peace and could feel the spirit lift and go by the time she was done with the prayer. Then I prayed for her as she also had Arnold Chiari Malformation for over ten years and had tried surgery which unfortunately did not work. After prayer she was healed and could move her head around without hearing a clicking sound. She also had a bulge on her upper back that shrank after prayer. Her lungs were healed from COPD and she could take deep breaths and walk without a problem and her stomach pain was healed and a leg grew out to match the other leg. She received a complete overhaul from the Lord and felt the best she had in many years. A couple months later she invited me back to do more ministry for family and neighbors. It was amazing because a couple of her neighbors had their family come over and they were from Noblesville near where I lived.

In July I attended a revival in Fort Wayne at First Assembly of God and met a 14 year old boy. He was a very sweet spirited boy who was born with his right foot flipped upside down so that he had to walk on the top of his foot. He went to Chicago to get major surgery to turn it over so he could walk on the bottom of the foot. As you can imagine there were a lot of complications with this procedure. He had back issues and his right leg was at least two inches shorter than his left and his right foot was shorter than his left. I love a good challenge and immediately commanded his back to be healed and corrected and it was and then I went after the leg to grow out which it did and the foot to grow out. Unfortunately after the leg grew out to be the same length and he walked around their prayer room the leg started to shrink back. So I commanded it to grow out again which it promptly did and he was able to walk around with it the same length. But then it shrank again. This went on for almost 2 hours as I was determined to keep the leg grown out and the same length. Finally it stayed out and he was able to run for the first time in his life.

Near the end of this battle a woman who worked at the church popped her head into the room to empty the trash and I noticed she had her arm in a sling. So I asked what was wrong and she said she just had torn rotator cuff surgery so I asked if I could pray and she would be completely healed in seconds and she said sure. So I said "rotator cuff be healed and all pain gone in Jesus name" and instantly she was healed and she was in shock as she really did not expect to be healed. She could move her arm all around in a circle with no pain at all. I went back to the 14 year old boy and his leg was finally staying out for more than ten minutes and I assumed his healing was complete. On Monday morning I received a call from his mother. She said they went to church on Sunday morning and he was able to stand the entire worship time without being tired and he testified as to what God did the night before in lengthening his leg and foot. Everyone was cheering for him and God. Then on their drive back home from church he normally could put his thumb and index finger around his ankle area on the leg that was skinnier. He noticed he could no longer touch his fingers around the circumference as his leg had begun to grow thicker to match the other leg. But on Monday morning his leg retracted back to being two inches shorter. His mother called me to pray over the phone for him which I did and his leg promptly grew out once again.

Over the next several days his leg continued this back and forth dance and when they called me and I prayed it grew back so I asked the Lord what in the world was happening as I had never seen anything like this before. The Lord told me the boy was going to pray for people and they would be healed so the enemy was trying to keep him from his destiny by stealing his healing so he would give up and never become what the Lord had for him. He told me to tell him to never give up and command his own leg to grow out and that once he knew his authority in Christ that the enemy would have to give up and his leg would stay out. So over the next week he commanded it to grow out whenever he noticed it had shrunken and immediately it would grow out. Finally the enemy gave up and the leg stayed out. What I am trying to get people to understand and realize is whatever your mountain is (back pain, a short leg, diabetes, stroke, cancer) that as long as you change your mind from fear and defeat into faith and authority your mountain MUST move. The enemy will not give up easily and most people give up before they see the breakthrough. This boy at age 14 was determined to see it through. How about you?

Just a few months later the boy decided to start praying for other people and they were being healed. He had a man that had a torn rotator cuff in his shoulder who did not believe he would be healed by the boy so when the boy prayed for it, the pain left instantly and the man was shocked he could move his arm without a problem. He became an instant believer that Jesus could heal but only through people of faith. What a great example of learning about your authority, taking the authority and not giving up. To God be the glory! People today give up too early and never see what they could do through Christ and so the enemy wins and they keep their sicknesses and diseases which grieves God and me.

Pastor Tim Brown of New Life Assembly of God wanted to visit the revival that was going on in Fort Wayne so we drove up early and went to Glenbrook Mall in the afternoon. I used to go to that mall when I was younger as it was always a treat and I had fun memories. Now it became a smorgasbord of opportunity for me to pray for random people in need of healing! The first person that caught my eye was a teenage boy who was wearing a cast on his left arm. I asked what happened and he said he was in an accident and had broken his forearm. I told him about all the healings that we were seeing and asked if I could pray for him and he said yes. So I just said "Arm be healed, pain be gone in Jesus name" and instantly he felt heat in his arm as the bone was being healed. He was amazed and very thankful. Then we found a young man that was wearing a protective soft boot on one foot so I asked him what happened and he said he had a torn Achilles. I told him we prayed for people and they got healed instantly so asked if we could heal him and he said yes. The Lord had me just point at his foot and say "Achilles heel be healed in Jesus name" and instantly he felt heat and was healed. I thought it was cool that I was able to pray by saying "heel be healed" as I had never said that before and it sounded funny. Then we came upon some teenagers and one boy had hurt his shoulder so I asked if we could pray and he actually said no. I pleaded with him and told him he would be healed instantly but he said "Nah, I'm good." It saddened me because I knew he would have been healed had he allowed us to pray. Then the Lord spoke to me telling me that he did not have the faith required. He said that all the faith he needed was to let me pray and He would have healed him instantly but because he did not even have the faith of a mustard seed he would not be healed. The Lord told me when Jesus was in his hometown, many people would not let Him pray for them either because they did not believe. He could heal them. Unfortunately today there are many that have no faith at all to even allow someone to pray for them. We continued on our way and healed about five other people over the next hour.

We went on to First Assembly of God in Ft. Wayne and looked for people there that needed healing. We immediately found an older woman who had pain in her lower back. Prayed three times for her before she became totally healed (sometimes the enemy wants us or the person you are praying for to give up before they see the healing manifest). I noticed a younger 40's looking woman who was watching us down the hallway from where we were and felt that she was going to ask us to be healed. Sure enough, as we walked down the hallway towards her she stopped us and said she noticed we had prayed and the woman was healed. She wanted us to pray for her and we said sure!

The woman had been through trauma with an automobile accident when she was fifteen and had progressively gotten worse with pain in her neck, shoulder, back and arm. At times it was debilitating to her so she was desperate for healing. So we prayed and instantly she felt heat come on her neck and back and shoulder and arm and all the pain left. No more burning pain for the first time in over 25 years. She was so thankful and grateful.

As we ate at the church I noticed a couple in their 80's that had pains in their feet and hands, prayed and they were instantly healed. It was so easy because God healed whoever we saw that needed healing.

In August of 2015 I was invited to attend Muncie's Christfest event with musical groups singing near downtown and when I arrived there were about 15 people in the prayer tent ready to pray for people but none came for prayer. Immediately the Lord told me that no one there actually believed they would be healed if they came into the tent and I needed to go out and find people who looked in pain and heal them. So the first person I found sitting in the audience had a soft boot on her foot and I asked her what happened; she had fractured her ankle bone. I prayed and she felt heat and immediately could walk on it with no pain. Then I found a young man who was wearing a sling who had tennis elbow pain. I prayed and he was instantly healed and threw away his sling. Yay, Jesus was really moving now! Then I was talking to a woman named Leah who wanted to see miracle healings and had heard from some others that when I prayed for people they would really be healed. So as I was sharing with her some of the miracles I had seen the previous months my friend Judy from Anderson walked up to me and said there was a man in the tent who really needed healing. Finally, the first person who actually had the faith to come into the tent for prayer!

I walked into the tent and learned that it was the man that drove me from an offsite church location and dropped me off at the event near downtown Muncie. His story was that 15 years ago he was assaulted by another man and had severely injured his lower spine to the point he was confined to a wheelchair initially after the trauma for two years. Now fifteen years later he could only walk bent over in constant pain and with a cane. Leah was excited to see a miracle occur after just minutes before having a conversation with me about it. There were five or six other people that were watching at the same time which is great because the higher the risk, the greater the reward for Jesus. So I commanded his spine to be healed and spoke to his posture to be straightened up and he started to stand up straight for the first time in fifteen years and everyone could see it before their eyes. Then I commanded some pain in his lower back and hips to go and after a few minutes he started to walk standing upright without his cane. Then I told him to run so he started to run back and forth behind the tent and now there were about 20-30 people clapping and cheering for him. Someone ran up and told the event coordinators what had just happened so they got up on stage where all the music performers were standing and announced that a man who could barely walk with a cane was healed and now is running around. So the next thing I knew we had a line of people that wanted me to pray for them in the tent. It was so amazing to see as the people finally had faith to believe they would be healed. Instead of me having to find all the people in pain they came looking for me. It was such an honor to have Jesus work through me; I just wanted to cry because it was so precious and amazing to see. Thank you Jesus!

I prayed for more people in the tent and they received healed backs, necks, stomachs, arms, legs, feet, emotional pain and other issues. Many wanted me to pray for them to receive the same anointing the Lord had on my life. I prayed for them to receive it but later the Lord told me there was a time of testing and tribulation each person would have to overcome before they would be able to see the same level of anointing. He said because I had been through some extreme, extreme, extreme (did I mention extreme?) trials and tribulations the past 6 years and did not give up but persevered, I had been rewarded with this higher level of anointing. Others would also have to press through a time of hardship and tribulation in their own lives to receive a strong anointing. If He gave everyone the same anointing just because they asked for it they would not be able to handle it and would result in pride to rise up in them. Each and every one must go through a time of testing and refining so they can be trusted to receive it yet they still could see people healed because of their faith. It made sense to me because I know had I just asked someone to give me the same level of anointing for an extremely high rate of healings without overcoming various difficult circumstances then my pride could have risen up inside of me.

There is something about going through a process of learning and overcoming obstacles in your life and not giving up and then finally receiving a reward that brings a much stronger level of satisfaction and gratitude than just getting a gift and not having to endure suffering or hardship. Think about it like this – if I gave my son $1 million dollars and he did not have to do anything for it, how grateful and humble would he be with managing it? He would most likely have it all spent within a year or less because it did not cost him any blood, sweat or tears to receive it and he would most likely move farther away from the Lord and closer to the world. Therefore I believe that when a person is truly ready to receive an increase in their anointing from the Lord, then the Lord will give it to them. I know when Robby Dawkins prayed over me to receive a double anointing, I can honestly say I was truly ready and was hungry for it in the spirit because of all that I had to endure. I had been through some extreme circumstances that very few human beings would have ever endured willingly. The Lord was ready to bless me with this gift due to my determination and not giving up no matter how hard the tribulation was. I had matured in the Lord and was extremely patient and could take whatever the enemy did to come against me. I would not be shaken. Can anyone pray for people and see them healed? Yes, but to do it at a very high rate consistently comes with a price. The enemy will try to come against you to stop you but you must overcome and never give up no matter what and continue to persist. Little by little you will see an even higher rate of success, and it is beyond the shadow of a doubt something special to see life changing healings.

Later in August, Pastor Tim Brown of New Life Assembly asked me again if I would start a Healing Room at his church. I prayed and the Lord said yes, now was the time. The Lord told me to start it in October and showed me a vision of signs posted all around Noblesville and Hamilton county talking about healing prayer every Saturday from 12-4. I had come from another church that had a healing room, but they went from twice a month for two hours at a time to just once a month for three hours so I was not sure if we could sustain doing healing every Saturday for four hours a day with the number of persons needed to pray for the healings. The Lord told me He would provide the prayer team members and bring people to the rooms that needed healing every week. He said not to worry about the details and when the people drove past my signs it would be a 'sign from the Lord' for them to come and be healed. He said people would come from all over Indiana to our rooms as the word got out. He also said to not limit the Holy Spirit and that we would see many people delivered from demonic spirits afflicting them.

Over Labor Day weekend a friend of mine asked me if I wanted to come to a large hospital in Indianapolis that he worked at and pray for nurses and staff. I was excited for the opportunity to see healing in the medical community. Of course! I told him, "I would love to pray for nurses and staff!" I visited the hospital over four separate days and began to heal the nurses and staff from all kinds of infirmities. We started in the basement and met a woman who had pain in her feet and there were several other nurses watching so after I prayed her feet did not hurt anymore. Next was a male nurse and he had significant back pain. After prayer he no longer had pain and was shocked. Then I prayed for a female nurse who had a leg shorter than the other and it grew out. Then a woman with some emotional pain over her husband needed one on one counseling and prayer which the Lord had me do.

We moved up a floor and there were many that had arthritis and immediately they began to get instantly healed. One nurse had pain and numbness in her thighs that she had for years and the doctors gave up on a cure. In seconds after prayer she could feel her thighs again and the pain that was deep inside was no more. Then other nurses that saw that she was healed nearby asked I pray for them and then they were getting healed from arthritis and back pain, and legs growing out.

Over the next few days it was so awesome to be able to pay back the nurses for all the things they do to help their patients. The hospital had not approved me to pray for the patients so I honored that and just loved on all the nurses and staff that needed healing. It was a great experience that I will always treasure.

Later in September, Pastor Tim Brown took a team with him to minister to an Assembly of God church in Attica, Indiana. Joe Swartz was with us and felt a pain in his neck, back, stomach and knees and asked if anyone in the church had those conditions. Interestingly a woman sitting near the back said she actually had all of those conditions. So she came up and I prayed for her neck and instantly it was healed. Next her back was healed in seconds. Then her stomach pain left. Finally her knees were knocked (they bent inward) and I commanded them to become straight and they were straightened. Then she received a word from the Lord and started crying as she was touched emotionally. It was such an awesome display of Jesus loving on her and so humbling to be a part of it.

Finally October 17, 2015 was approaching when we were starting our first day of the Healing Rooms. Here we go – we had no idea who was going to show up or how they would hear about us. My good friend Joe Swartz shocked me by saying he wanted to donate to help promote the kickoff of the Healing Rooms. I told him that I really needed at least $250 to do some promotion with signs and radio ads so he wrote me a check on the spot and handed it to me. As I was driving back home that night the Lord told me to look at the check. I responded with "Why? The check is for $250." He said no it was more. I opened it up and was shocked that it was for $1,000! I was so grateful to the Lord and to Joe for his obedience and faithfulness! So I advertised on a Christian station 98.7 FM from Anderson for several weeks and the Lord said to also advertise on secular radio, so I chose the top station in Indianapolis WZPL 99.5 FM as well as a top mix music station WNTR 107.9 FM. The Lord had given me a vision in August on the way to church at New Life Assembly of God in Noblesville where I saw signs posted along the streets and roads and when people drove past them that they would know it was a sign from the Lord for them to come and be healed. So I purchased 16 signs to post around town. It was all coming together now. My dream ever since reading the John G. Lake book was coming to pass. To have the first healing room in Indiana that was open every week to the public for 4 or more hours every Saturday. Thank you Lord!

One of our first to come into our Healing Rooms was a twenty-something young man that had come in with extreme pain in his abdomen and back. He had been suffering for several days in bed and the doctor said he needed a colonoscopy. He said he almost thought about going to the emergency room at the hospital but wanted to give God a chance to heal him. So he came in and I commanded the pain in the stomach to be gone and immediately he felt all pain leave him. Then prayed for the back and it was healed. He then went out to the sanctuary in the church and began to run around and jump as he had no pain at all. Yay, Jesus loves to heal!

November 7th I was invited to go to a men's retreat at Camp Tecumseh north of Lafayette by Pastor Owen Mason. A man named Juan from Puerto Rico was there who suffered from severe back pain from an incurable disease called Spondylosis. It was a disc disease that caused his discs to degenerate over time and he had suffered with it for 20 years. He used to have to sleep in reclining chairs with heating pads and also took pain killers all the time but still could not get relief. After praying for him a total of three times his pain left completely and he could touch his toes. He was already scheduled for an MRI the following Monday so he went to his doctor and sure enough the results showed he had completely new discs in his back. He could run and exercise and felt perfect and his life was changed in seconds. All Glory to God!

On November 21st a young man named Tyler who had visited and was healed a month before came hobbling into our Healing Rooms. He had fallen on his right knee and felt a lot of pain. He had been prayed for by several people but did not get healed. So I was excited to see him and up to the challenge. We had a couple of our team members pray for him but he was still in pain. So I decided to pray for him and after a couple prayers he was running around the sanctuary in no pain at all. He persevered and did not give up as he wanted to take his healing and not allow his pain to win.

The word started to get around and we began receiving people from Muncie, Lafayette, north of Kokomo, Greenwood, Mooresville, even Bloomington, Auburn and Fort Wayne which confirmed what the Lord told me back in August, that we would have people drive from all over the state of Indiana to our rooms to be healed and delivered. We began to see many more healings and also began to see people delivered from spirits like Jezebel and Leviathan. Many were thankful and grateful to us and some donated $100 as they were finally free from a lifetime of pain and divorces. Couples began to visit who were ready for divorce and we were able to set one of the spouses free from Jezebel and save their marriage. The Lord said that He wanted these Healing Rooms to be exactly what Jesus did and said for us to do in Matthew 10:8 NKJV *"Heal the sick, cleanse the lepers, raise the dead, cast out demons. Freely you have received, freely give."*

We started to notice that more than half of those that came into our rooms for physical infirmities had a spiritual component behind the pain. When you have spirits that are causing pain what do you do? You command them to be gone in the name of Jesus. So many of those that came in needed to read renunciation prayers to break off generational curses and then they began to feel much better without prayer for the physical pains to go. Also when people commanded the spirits of Jezebel and Leviathan to go they noticed that their back and shoulder pains went away. Many did not realize that they could be living under curses from these spirits that were afflicting them their entire life. We discovered many whose fathers or grandfathers were involved with Freemasons and Shriners who speak secret oaths against Jesus Christ and to the Great Architect of the Universe which is code for Satan. Thus they had been living under the curse of Leviathan and would suffer back and neck pain their whole lives. Many were innocent wives or children of those involved in such secret covenants. It was a true revelation for those that came to us as no other healing room in the state addressed the reality of what was going on spiritually with them. Either other healing ministries did not know how to address it or were afraid of offending someone. God told me to not be afraid and speak the truth in love and the Holy Spirit would guide all of our deliverances and it would be greatly appreciated. Everyone who has come to our Rooms has been thankful and grateful for having us share the truth with them. Yay, Jesus loves to heal through us!

I have prayed for five couples (that I am aware of) who wanted to become pregnant but could not, who subsequently became pregnant after prayer. Some of them became pregnant within a week after prayer. The possibilities of using the authority of Christ to bless others are endless if you think about it. Is there a minimum age for a child to pray for others? Do you have to be at the age of accountability (13 or 14) in order to operate in the authority of Christ? Is there just a Junior Holy Spirit available to children to do miracles?

One Wednesday evening at New Life Assembly of God the pastor's ten year old daughter had an ankle injury that she asked me to pray for. So I prayed and had her start walking on it but she received no relief. So I prayed a second time and still she had no relief. This seemed highly unusual as she usually received healing very quickly in the past. So I prayed a third time and still no relief. Finally the Lord spoke to me and showed me a seven year old girl that was watching what was happening and said He wanted her to heal the ten year old because she was going to be very gifted in healing and He wanted her to start now. I instructed the seven year old to pray and instantly the ankles were healed. During the worship service the Lord told me that He wanted her to serve in our Healing Rooms. Later that weekend, the seven year old girl was playing in her backyard swinging with a twelve year old girl who jumped out of the swing and twisted her ankle. So the seven year old went up to the twelve year old and prayed over her ankle and instantly the pain left and she was healed. The older girl looked at her and said "How did you do that?" The younger girl said she had done it earlier that week for another girl and that it was easy. I love it! Later the next week the seven year old came in to our Healing Rooms and prayed for a man that had driven through the snow from Muncie. She prayed for several pains in his body and he was healed.

There are very few places in Indiana where people will do what Jesus said to do because they are afraid of what people will think or say. Well I am not afraid or ashamed to do what Jesus said and people are coming to our Healing Rooms because the Holy Spirit is not limited in any way. When you take yourself and fear out of the equation there is nothing that the Lord will not do. Some ministries are afraid to tell people they have demonic spirits afflicting them causing them to be addicted or depressed and doing things that they should not be doing. Why? Because they are afraid of what people will think and do not want to offend them. If they just ignore deliverance and pray for their physical pains to go, then did they do their job even if the afflicted are not healed or they only receive temporary relief? Jesus was not afraid to command spirits out of people in love and neither are we!

If you are a pastor or counselor in a church and you do not know how to deal with a person being tormented by addictions or behavior contrary to the Lord and you are afraid to make the person aware they could have a demonic presence, if they end up divorced, you share the responsibility (to whom much is given, much is required). The top reason people divorce is due to the enemy afflicting their lives. The sooner people realize that their issues are not with their spouse but with the spirits afflicting them, the sooner we will see people staying married, healed and becoming who they should be in Christ. When a person goes from spouse to spouse to spouse and never gets true deliverance there is something seriously wrong with

96

them and the church. Enough is enough – it is time to do what Jesus said to do and get out of the way and let the Holy Spirit direct! God is tired of seeing His people obliterated by the enemy as pastors turn a blind eye to the obvious! Learn your authority and know that demons are real. Christians can and do have demons that afflict them and it is time for them to be delivered and set free once and for all so they can have true love, joy and peace in their lives. Do not confuse God's unconditional love for His condoning actions that are contrary to His word. If you choose to sin or abuse then you will suffer consequences in life in order to wake you up to change and receive freedom. Hurting people hurt people and healed people heal people.

Chapter 8

Cancer Healed at Last

January 3, 2016 I attended Pastor Owen Mason's Church Alive in Lafayette. He let me pray over everyone that wanted prayer and it took over three hours after the service to pray for all that wanted healing. A seventeen year old girl that had sprained and fractured her ankles numerous times playing basketball was one of the people that wanted healing as she had a lot of pain in the ankles and had limited mobility. As I put my hands on her feet (and she was wearing socks) the Lord told me to keep my hands on her feet longer than the usual five or ten seconds that I commanded the healing to take place. It turned out to be about two minutes that I left my hands on her feet. It felt like my hands were getting blown on from a fan above me so I looked up and the only ceiling fan in the church was at least twenty feet away so I knew it could not be a breeze created by it. For the entire two minutes I felt a breeze on my hands that seemed cool. I asked the girl what she was feeling on her ankles and she said it felt as if they were in a bucket of ice as they were very cold. After two minutes I asked her to move her feet around and see how they felt. She said that she could not feel any pain at all. She peeled her right sock down and gasped, "My scar is gone!" She did not tell me that she had a scar on her ankle and I did not pray for it. So it was a very sweet creative miracle that Jesus did by taking her scar completely away. She also had pain in her jaw for some time and after prayer she no longer heard a clicking sound and had no more pain. Yay Jesus!

Up until this point in my life, I had never had anyone ask me to pray for healing cancer and I felt in my spirit the time had finally arrived for cancer to fall. On January 6, 2016 it was time. I attended church that Wednesday night at New Life Assembly of God in Noblesville and Pastor Tim Brown was speaking. Shortly after we started worshipping I received a direct message on Facebook (I love how God is using social media more and more to connect people). The message was from a friend from Warsaw, Indiana of my brother Chris Schuman. He sent me a message that he had heard from my brother that I had seen many healings in the past year and he would like for me to pray for his seven year old son. He said his son had non-Hodgkin's childhood Lymphoma and was scheduled for surgery the next morning. He said a woman that did not know him approached him the previous Sunday at church after they heard a message about how God called Abraham to put his son Isaac on the altar. He said she told him that she was drawn to him to pray that he would not turn his back on God from something that was about to happen. Based on that word he was very worried that his son was going to die during surgery scheduled for Thursday morning and he hoped he would be able to handle it if God took his son. He asked me for my thoughts and if I would pray. I messaged him back on Facebook that God never would take his son from him and only the enemy does that. Jesus wants to heal us but cannot do it if we are in fear and worry as we need to command the healing with the authority he gave us in Jesus name. I told him I would call him later that night. Pastor Tim started preaching and the Lord told me to go right then to pray for the boy and not to wait until after church was over as the boy would be going to bed. So I wrote a note to my good friend Bob Mann on the back of an offering envelope letting him know why I was leaving the service. See the note below:

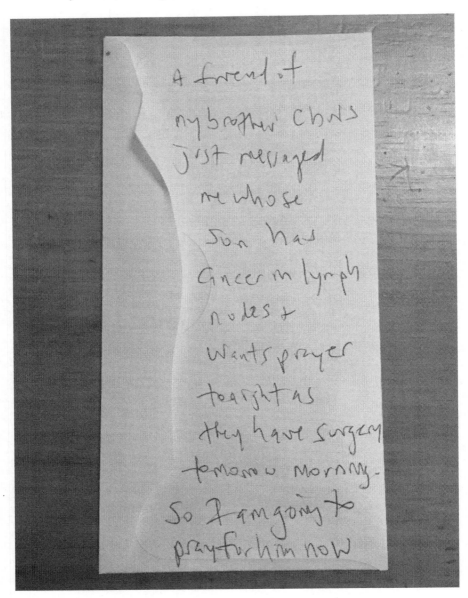

I felt strongly in my spirit that this was already a done deal because he was an innocent seven year old boy that Jesus was waiting to heal but could only do it if we commanded it and it was going to be a good training lesson for the boy's father as to how healing worked.

So I left the service and walked to the basement of the church into a private room and called the boy's father. I explained briefly how I learned about healing and anyone can do it but they first need to know their authority in Christ. When you pray you command the healing, just like Christ and the enemy would have to go. The father told me that his son had first developed the non-Hodgkin's Lymphoma cancer when he was just five and went through treatment for it. They thought they got it all and the doctors said there was only a 10% chance of it coming back. Then in November of 2015 it came back and it was indeed cancerous again so now they were planning on risky surgery because of a six inch rock hard mass on his neck that was protruding about half the width of a golf ball. I told his son to get ready to be healed! I would say a very short prayer and he would feel some heat on his neck and then it would dissolve and be gone. He was very excited to finally have God heal him of the annoying cancer. So I told the father to place his hands on his son's neck and I would say a very short prayer then he would feel heat and the cancer would be gone. He put his hands on the boys neck and then I commanded "Lymph nodes be healed, cancer be gone in Jesus name." Then I waited a few seconds and asked the son how he felt and he said "I feel happy!" His father said his son's neck felt really, really hot and the cancer mass was dissolving. Within less than a minute the cancer bulge was completely gone. Yay Jesus! His father's hands were trembling as he was amazed at what he just witnessed.

The the next day he took his son to his surgery and the doctor looked at his son and could not find the bulge on his neck anymore. He had just seen his son two days before and asked the father where the bulge went (I would have loved to have seen the expression on the doctor's face!). His father said "Well we had a guy from Indianapolis pray for him over the phone and then his neck got hot and the bulge dissolved." The doctor looked incredulous. Then he decided to proceed with the surgery to see what was still inside his neck, if anything. All he could find that was left was a little mushy thing and told the boy's father that he was 99% sure the cancer was completely gone. Yay Jesus – all the glory! The doctor sent the small mushy thing off to a lab in Tennessee to be tested for all kinds of cancer. A week later the results came back and showed Jesus got it all and there were no signs of cancer in it. Praise the Lord!

The lesson to be learned is that had the father listened to the mysterious woman at church and stayed in worry and fear the cancer would have never have been healed and something worse could have happened. Instead of getting into fear he decided to do something about it. When he had heard from his good friend Chris that his brother prayed for people and they were getting healed, he activated his faith at that point and contacted me. That's when Jesus was ready to heal as soon as the words were spoken to command the cancer gone. This is how it works – by taking our authority and commanding the healing to occur and sickness and pain to go. This is why it is so critical for people to learn their authority and know it so when they have people that need healing they will allow Jesus to heal through them. Asking God to heal does not usually work. Pleading with God to heal does not work. He has already given us the necessary tools to heal by the blood of Jesus. Commanding the healing to occur in Jesus name does work.

I was so excited to see and experience someone who had cancer ask for prayer and see them healed. I was especially excited that the boy lived 100 miles away and the prayer was effective over the phone so that others would see there was no reason that could stop the effectiveness of a prayer over the phone, even thousands of miles away. I was ready to see cancer fall after seeing hundreds of other non-cancerous healings that I had witnessed the previous 8 months. 2016 was off to a great start and the Lord told me to expect to see thousands healed the rest of the year from anything and everything.

January 23, 2016 we had a woman from Elwood who learned about our Healing Rooms on the internet. She found out in November 2015 that she had stage 3 cancer in her lungs. People all around her had sickness of their own and were very discouraging and negative by their lack of support of her. She wanted to find people that believed she could be healed and was very excited to see there is a church north of Indianapolis that actually believed in healing and saw healings every week. So she came to the rooms expecting to be healed. Again I just prayed "Lungs be healed, cancer be gone in Jesus name" and she felt she was healed. On February 3rd she had a CT scan that confirmed her lungs had no cancer in them any longer. She came back to our church and testified before the entire congregation on Sunday, February 7th that Jesus healed her (and visiting Prophets Kathie Walters and Bonnie Jones were in attendance that Sunday). It was a very special moment for all that were there and a great tribute to what Jesus could do when we stay in faith and stay out of fear. Everyone clapped and cheered and Jesus got all the glory!

We had many that came to our Healing Rooms that had suffered from a father that was harsh and not loving. When a lack of love from one's father enters the equation, this sets them up for a lifetime of pain and heartache and is truly a sad situation to have to endure. Their life becomes centered on receiving approval and if they do not receive it they felt guilt, shame and condemnation. They suffer much rejection from others (spouses, managers at work, pastors, etc), and as a result they constantly seek approval from God and from others. They struggle in their life and circumstances constantly and never feel at peace or rest. They strive to be perfect and are driven to succeed and accomplish what they want at all cost. Perfectionism is also a spirit that is under the control of the spirit of Leviathan. Physical manifestations of Leviathan are a sore neck and shoulder area, due to carrying tension in their body most of the time. So as they would command the spirit to go, their pain would be healed.

We also saw many needed to break off generational curses from their family line. This is why medical doctors ask you what diseases run in your family because if your grandfather and great grandfather suffered from a certain disease, then so could you. We also saw quite a few people that had the Jezebel spirit which is comprised of the spirits of control, manipulation and deception and is quite common with women that are not loved by their father and feel rejected (and can also affect men if their fathers treat them harshly and they never felt that they could get their approval). Deliverance from spirits is a very common thing that Jesus said we would do and from my experience is a very loving thing to do for someone that has no idea why they are behaving the way they are and have broken relationships. When a spirit has a right to co-exist in your body it will cause you to do things that are not good for you and ultimately can inflict your body with pain until you are set free from them. Demons are real and need to be dealt with or a Christian will forever be afflicted and often times the only way they can deal with it is to be medicated their entire lives which is not what the Lord wants for them. I have never had to raise my voice to anyone that had a demonic spirit because when you know your authority in Christ it has to go. We lead people through prayers where they command the spirits to be gone and it is a very calm process that is awesome to watch as the person becomes free for the first time.

The Lord started connecting me with the medical community and counseling groups that did not know how to fix people that were having serious issues outside of their expertise and needed a supernatural healing from the Lord. In early March of 2016 I had a Christian medical doctor who I knew from a previous church that started to refer certain patients to me that had issues that only God could heal. Some had demonic influences that were manifesting as out of control behavior. I also met with a well respected Christian chiropractor who had one of the largest practices in central Indiana who was connected to me through a mutual friend. He was very interested in how God was using me and the Healing Rooms to miraculously heal people from all kinds of affliction. When he works on various patients that have cancer and other infirmities that his practice cannot fix, he would refer those patients to me and I would see them at the Healing Rooms. Another chiropractor asked to meet with me as he was also interested in the Healing Rooms. The Lord told me that the results would speak for themselves and as more people became aware of the results that it would continue to grow. People are hungry for the real thing and God wants to heal His people perfectly so that He can have relationship with them and save them from a life of hell. So what better way of telling them that He loves them than to heal them.

What will the remainder of 2016 and beyond hold? I would say that we will see more and more people healed and brought to the Lord through His love and mercy for us. More people who are already Christians will want to learn how they can heal other people and pass it on. The Healing Rooms at New Life Assembly of God, 698 N. 10th Street in Noblesville are currently open every Saturday from 12-4 (and I can see the hours expanding as well as the number of days each week as we see an increase in people becoming aware of them). The Lord wants to train people that have a genuine interest in becoming stronger in their own healing anointing by allowing them to observe. From 1915-20's John G. Lake had his healing rooms open 6 days a week in Spokane, Washington and later started them in Portland, Oregon and later down the California coast and that would be a dream of mine to replicate. Our Healing Room team is now being asked more and more to go to other churches around Indiana to conduct healing miracle nights which is always exciting seeing someone healed for the first time as their eyes light up when they feel their bodies get hot or tingling or even cold and all their pain goes away instantly. I see people coming from all over the Midwest to be healed and other towns and cities will have people that the Lord has called to start healing rooms in their local churches. I had one man who flew in to see me from Raleigh, North Carolina to receive prayer as his former wife abused him strongly as she had the Jezebel spirit. We are also now seeing medical doctors, nurses chiropractors and psychologists referring their most challenging patients to our Healing Rooms.

Chapter 9

Common Misconceptions

When I grew up I had no idea how healing worked as I never saw anyone healed instantly after they were prayed for. I believed some things that were not true and was confused on other scriptures so I believe it is important to better understand some of the confusion that I and others have had.

Paul asked for God to take away his 'Thorn in the Flesh' but God said no. So if God would not heal Paul then he probably wants me to be in pain and endure for His gain as well.

Let us take a look specifically at that scripture in the Bible. 2 Corinthians 12:7-9 NKJV *"⁷And lest I should be exalted above measure by the abundance of the revelations, a thorn in the flesh was given to me, a messenger of Satan to buffet me, lest I be exalted above measure. [8]Concerning this thing I pleaded with the Lord three times that it might depart from me. [9]And He said, 'My grace is sufficient for you, for My strength is made perfect in weakness'. Therefore most gladly I will rather boast in my infirmities, that the power of Christ may rest upon me."*

So what are the words in this verse that could not be misconstrued concerning a physical sickness? How about '*a thorn in the flesh was given to me, a messenger of Satan to buffet me*'?

A "messenger of Satan" in the Greek translation refers to someone who is sent and denotes a definite personality. This same word for messenger is translated in other verses of the New Testament as "angel." Angels, as God's messengers, are created beings with personalities. Satan's messengers also known as 'demons' would be in the same category. Sickness is not a personality, nor a messenger. It is a being and the logical explanation is that it is a demonically afflicted human being who was sent by Satan to buffet or harass Paul wherever he speaks and ministers in various towns and cities. Buffet means to strike repeatedly. God does not send demonic spirits against people in the Body of Christ. God sent the Holy Spirit and has given us His Word, which is profitable for doctrine, for reproof, for correction and instruction in righteousness to discipline and to guide us. The demon afflicted person was assigned to Paul for one reason – to stop the Word from being preached. Wherever Paul went the messenger of Satan worked to incite the people against him.

Paul's thorn was a person sent by Satan who caused him great irritation, but not with sickness or disease. In 2 Corinthians 11:23-27 NKJV, Paul lists the infirmities to which he is referring: "*[23]Are they ministers of Christ? – I speak as a fool – I am more: in labors more abundant, in stripes above measure, in prisons more frequently, in deaths often. [24] From the Jews five times I received forty stripes minus one. [25] Three times I was beaten with rods; once I was stoned; three times I was shipwrecked; a night and a day I have been in the deep; [26] in journeys often, in perils of water, in perils of robbers, in perils of my own countrymen, in perils of the Gentiles, in perils in the city, in perils in the wilderness, in perils in the sea, in perils among fast brethren;* ^{27} *in weariness and toil, in sleeplessness often, in hunger and thirst, in fastings often, in cold and nakedness".*

The saying of "thorn in the flesh" is a figure of speech or illustration. It is similar today to calling someone who irritates us a "pain in the neck." Review the below Old Testament scriptures that refer to the saying of 'thorn in the side or eyes':

Numbers 33:55 NKJV says *"But if you do not drive out the inhabitants of the land from before you, then it shall be that those whom you let remain shall be irritants in your eyes and <u>thorns in your sides</u>, and they shall harass you in the land where you dwell."*

It is obvious in this scripture that the term 'thorns in your sides' is similar to our saying today of 'pain in the neck' and does not refer to an actual physical sickness or disease.

Also in Joshua 23:11-13 NKJV (Joshua speaking to the elders, judges, and officers of Israel) *"*^{11} *Therefore take careful heed to yourselves, that you love the Lord your God.* ^{12} *Or else, if indeed you do go back, and cling to the remnant of these nations – these that remain among you – and make marriages with them, and go in to them and they to you,* ^{13} *know for certain that the Lord your God will no longer drive out these nations from before you. But they shall be snares and traps to you, and scourges on your sides and <u>thorns in your eyes</u>, until you perish from this good land which the Lord your God has given you."*

Once again the saying of thorns is referring to a pain in the neck for them. Then in Judges 2:1-4 (the Angel of the Lord was speaking to the Israelites) NKJV *"*^{1}*Then the Angel of the Lord came up from Gilgal to Bochim, and said: "I led you up from Egypt and brought you to the land of which I swore to your fathers; and I said, 'I will never break My covenant with you* ^{2}*and you shall make no covenant with the inhabitants of this land; you shall tear down their altars, but you have not obeyed My voice. Why have you done this?* ^{3}*Therefore I also said; 'I will not drive them out before you; but they shall be <u>thorns in your side</u>, and their gods shall be a snare to you.'* ^{4}*So it*

108

was, when the Angel of the Lord spoke these words to all the children of Israel, that the people lifted up their voices and wept."

I pray to God asking him to heal me and other people but they never get healed. Isn't it up to God if someone gets healed?

God wants to heal all His people of every sickness and disease but what did Jesus say on the matter? Did he say to ask and plead with God to heal or did he say we were to command the healings and other mountains (problems) in our lives like He did?

Mark 11:23-24 NKJV says *"23For assuredly, I say to you, whoever says to this mountain, 'Be removed and be cast into the sea,' and does not doubt in his heart, but believes that those things he says will be done, he will have whatever he says. 24"Therefore I say to you, whatever things you ask when you pray, believe that you receive them, and you will have them."*

So how many times did Jesus state the word 'says' in verse 23 above? Three times. So from that verse it is clear that we are to say the words with authority expecting what we say to manifest in the physical. The enemy knows if you know your authority and if he has to back off or not based upon it. So if I were to have prayed like I usually prayed for my toothache I would have said "Please God heal my tooth – if it be thy will." Do you think that lines up with what Jesus instructed us to do and it would have made the spirit of infirmity or pain go from my mouth? I don't think so! I took authority and commanded it to go and it left instantly. 90% of the healings I see in someone I pray for happen instantly while some take a few prayers to successfully break the enemy's hold on them. If the person has some things that they need to do (i.e. forgive someone, renounce the spirit of Jezebel or Leviathan or other spirit) then that could prohibit their healing from occurring. Once the prayer is commanded then one just needs to thank Jesus that they are healed and expect it to manifest whether it takes a day, week, month or year. I have been healed every time from every affliction and sometimes it happened instantly, sometimes in two days and sometimes over a month. Sometimes the Lord wants those we are praying for to do some work on their part as He wants them to learn about their authority. Those that are not saved are the easiest to get healed because the Lord knows that they do not know their authority so when we pray for them they are usually healed instantly. Once we are a believer then we could believe things that are not correct or if we have any hidden sin we need to be honest with the Lord and deal with the truth and not have anything that could stop the Lord from doing the healing.

What if I have unforgiveness towards someone that hurt me – can that give me a sickness and prevent my healing?

What does the word say about this?

Matthew 6:14-15 NKJV says *[14] "For if you forgive men their trespasses, your heavenly Father will also forgive you. 16 "But if you do not forgive men their trespasses, neither will your Father forgive your trespasses."*

If we are a Christian and have unforgiveness towards someone we can definitely open up a door to the enemy to come in and bring sickness and disease upon us. We need to forgive everyone for whatever they have done to us and take no offense against them.

Proverbs 19:11 The Message *"Smart people know how to hold their tongue; their grandeur is to forgive and forget."*

Colossians 3:13-14 NKJV *[13] "bearing with one another, and forgiving one another, if anyone has a complaint against another; even as Christ forgave you, so you also must do. [14] But above all these things put on love, which is the bond of perfection."*

When you forgive you do not exonerate or excuse the person for what they did but you free yourself and ultimately feel better inside. Many people have a lot of physical issues that develop in them as they grew up with an unloving father or mother or had a spouse that divorced them and retained the anger and hurt inside them causing stomach ulcers, high blood pressure, heart issues and other sickness. Until they truly forgive they will have many issues that have a right to stay on them. So always be quick to forgive and give them to God and let Him deal with the sin in their lives while you enjoy a life full of love and peace and freedom.

I know that God can heal but maybe he wants to teach me something through this sickness, disease or pain.

The only thing I ever learned though a sickness, disease or pain is that I felt horrible. Paul states in 1 Peter 2:24 NKJV *"who Himself bore our sins in His own body on the tree, that we, having died to sins, might live for righteousness – by whose stripes you were healed."*

Therefore Jesus died on the cross and when he was scourged we were healed.

The only scripture that I can find in the New Testament where God will bring sickness on someone is in Revelation 2:21-23 NKJV *"21* *"And I gave her time to repent of her sexual immorality, and she did not repent.* *22 "Indeed I will cast her into a sickbed, and those who commit adultery with her into great tribulation, unless they repent of their deeds. 23 I will kill her children with death, and all the churches shall know that I am He who searches the minds and hearts. And I will give to each one of you according to your works."*

This refers to people in church today that have the Jezebel spirit (comprised of spirits of control, manipulation, lying, false teaching, etc) and are teaching people false things that cause them to stumble. God will put them on a sickbed and kill their children (which are those that they teach their false doctrine to who ascribe to their teachings and become like them operating in the Jezebel spirit). An example may be if someone were to teach that God is such a loving God that if you end up going to hell he will not allow you to burn in the lake of fire forever. He will take you and put you some other place that is not as torturous or He will just burn you up so you do not feel pain. Or if someone says that Christians cannot be affected by demons. Or there is no such thing as the Jezebel spirit. I have seen people that operate with the Jezebel spirit literally getting sicker and in more pain if they deny they have the spirit and choose to keep it. One man's wife has almost died several times and refuses to renounce Jezebel. God is serious when He puts you on notice and you still choose to keep that spirit.

So, yes sickness and disease can teach you that you better draw closer to the Lord and learn about His ability to keep you healthy but if God is putting it on you to teach you something then why would you pray for Him to heal you? Just let the disease play its course and die. I am being facetious here but it is a logical conclusion if you think God is trying to teach you something as it would be a waste of time to pray to take it away early.

I have sinned a lot so God must be punishing me with sickness.

If God wanted to punish you due to your sin then He would just kill you and be done with it. He wants as many to come to Christ and be saved as possible because He loves people. What tends to happen is that the reason people are sinning is they have been hurt by the enemy through their fathers or mothers or they never were encouraged to develop their faith with the Lord and to have a personal relationship with the Heavenly Father. What I have seen in my life is that when I pray for non-believers in God they are usually much easier to be healed because the Lord wants them to know that He did it for them because He loves them. Therefore after I pray for them and they get healed they ask "How did you do that?" and then I tell them Jesus loves them and wants them to be healthy and to have a personal relationship with Him and then they could do the same miracles to help others. Many actually give their lives to the Lord after they are healed. What better evangelism tool than to heal an unbeliever of a disease or pain as they know they did not deserve it and they were not worthy so they will be hungry to learn all about Jesus the healer and how they can do the same for others.

The only time I have ever heard of God causing anyone more pain is told to us in the New Testament when he referred to Jezebel in Revelation chapter two. Obviously when a believer has hidden sin that they want to keep then they can open themselves up to all kinds of affliction.

God wants to keep me humble and sick so I totally depend on Him

God does want us to be humble and depend on Him but why would sickness encourage that? Sickness just makes us feel sick and we are not able to do what the Lord wants us to do and that is to help heal others, love on them and bring more into the Kingdom of God. Humbleness is a condition of future increase in blessings and receiving more spiritual gifts. If we become prideful then we need to remember what caused Lucifer to be kicked out of heaven was that he wanted to be just like God. So why would sickness be a wise way of keeping us humble?

Sickness is from the enemy meant to hurt us and God wants us healthy so that we can do more for His kingdom. John 10:10-11 NKJV *"10 The thief does not come except to steal, and to kill, and to destroy. I have come that they may have life, and that they may have it more abundantly. 11 I am the good shepherd. The good shepherd gives His life for the sheep."*

Do I have authority to cast out all demons from people that are afflicted by them? What if the people do not want them to go?

If you know your authority you will be able to cast out many demons just like Jesus said but some will not come out except by prayer and fasting and some we have no authority to cast out because of the free will of the person who may want to keep the demons.

In Matthew 10:1 ESV, *"And he called to him his twelve disciples and gave them authority over unclean spirits, to cast them out, and to heal every disease and every affliction."*

So this clearly states that Jesus gave the disciples authority to command demons to go from people and heal their diseases and affliction. So when you get this revelation into your spirit you will also be able to do the same thing. It will take time to truly know that you know that you have this authority as little victories will lead to larger victories.

Are there some demons that are stronger than your authority and what about a person that does not want them to come out?

Reading Matthew 17:14-21 NKJV *"14 And when they had come to the multitude, a man came to Him, kneeling down to Him and saying, 15 'Lord, have mercy on my son, for he is an epileptic and suffers severely; for he often falls into the fire and often into the water. 16 So I brought him to Your disciples, but they could not cure him'. 17 Then Jesus answered and said, 'O faithless and perverse generation, how long shall I be with you? How long shall I bear with you? Bring him here to Me.' 18 And Jesus rebuked the demon, and it came out of him; and the child was cured from that very hour. 19 Then the disciples came to Jesus privately and said, 'Why could we not cast it out?' 20 So Jesus said to them, "Because of your unbelief, for assuredly, I say to you, if you have faith as a mustard seed, you will say to this mountain, 'Move from here to there' and it will move; and nothing will be impossible for you. 21 However, this kind does not go out except by prayer and fasting."*

In my experience I have seen much success over children still living at home to command the spirits out as long as their parents want them to be delivered. For people that are living on their own they would need to want to be set free as they have their own free will. It may be hard to distinguish who really wants to be delivered by how crazy the spirit is making them behave.

It has been my experience with those who are tormented with the Jezebel and Leviathan spirits that they will have to command the spirits out themselves as no one can override their wills, thus it is extremely hard to get these people delivered. I have been very successful getting people delivered from them when I explain to them that they were unfortunately hurt through unloving and controlling fathers and/or mothers, that they did nothing wrong but get hurt and the spirit developed in thebehavingm as they moved into their teenage years and beyond. Then if they do not command the spirits to go, their lives will become more challenging as the Lord brings circumstances in their lives to make them want to get rid of the spirit. You can learn much more about the Jezebel and Leviathan spirits and how to get free from them through my book *Restored To Freedom*.

Kenneth E. Hagin gave a story in his book *The Believers Authority* that explains the free will of a person quite well when it comes to casting out demons. He was attending a church and they had a line of people that he was praying for one right after the other. When he came to one woman in line for prayer – who had a problem of behaving similarly to that of a woman in a trance or zombie-like state - the Lord stopped him before he prayed for her as He told him some things about her so Hagin told the woman (and her husband who was a deacon in the church) that he would talk with them privately in the senior pastor's office after he was done praying for everyone else. Later in the pastor's office he explained to the husband of the woman (with the woman looking on standing next to her husband) that the Lord told him that the woman had wanted to hear voices ever since she heard that Oral Roberts could hear from the Lord. He asked the woman if that was true and she said yes. Then Hagin said that unfortunately the voices that she heard were from demons and not the Lord as she wanted to hear these voices. Unfortunately she still wanted to hear these demonic voices so there was nothing that Hagin could do to override her free will to command the spirits out from her. Her husband was very sad, but Hagin said unfortunately some spirits can stay in the person due to the desire of that person to have them remain and no one who knows their authority or is greatly anointed can do anything about it.

I have met a few people that hear voices very clearly and I know that they are not from the Lord. Unfortunately the person wanted to continue having them present and so when I commanded them to leave they did not have to go and remained. They caused the person to do things to themselves which were not good or healthy causing them to be addicted to various stimulants. So in those cases we just have to continue to pray that the person will come to the end of themselves and hit bottom and want the demons to go. At that point they or we can command them gone and they will go.

Chapter 10

How to Walk in Christ's Authority

I believe this is the most important chapter in my book because what good is a healing if you later get another infirmity and do not know how to command it to be gone and stand in faith until you see it gone. I had heard at one time that over 50% of those that were healed when attending miracle healing nights at Benny Hinn conferences lost their healings within a couple of weeks or months. It was because the people that were healed never knew their authority in Christ to stand against the enemy when a symptom returned. Though they were healed of an infirmity they could not keep the healing because when the symptom returned they said to themselves "I guess it did not work." They did not know that they had the authority to command it gone for themselves and they really needed to know that.

The Lord told me that He wanted to make sure that everyone that I had personally healed was told they could lose it if the enemy brought back symptoms and they did not know their authority and how to stand strong against it. He made it very clear to me that ultimately everyone needed to learn about their own authority in Christ against all sickness and disease but unfortunately not all would press in and spend time to learn about it so the enemy would be able to give them additional infirmities. He said that everyone had to learn their own faith in their authority in Christ and if they did not want to spend the time in learning about it then the enemy could definitely hit them again with the same thing or something else. If not prepared for battle they can lose their healing and ultimately their lives.

So, yes this is a life or death battle that we all are in and if you do not know that you know your authority in Christ then the enemy will be able to defeat you. Therefore please do yourself a huge favor and spend time learning about your authority in Christ and expect to be tested by the enemy. You can defeat him every time if you do not give up. Like the 14 year old boy near Muncie, IN that I described earlier in this book. He fought for his authority day after day until the enemy finally gave up on shrinking the length of his leg back to where it started. It took him several weeks of battling before he finally won, but through his persistence and not giving up he won the fight. Your battle may not be that pronounced but what if you were afraid of getting bronchitis and pneumonia every year because you did not know your authority, and then one winter you caught it and subsequently died. This is serious stuff and I cannot state strongly enough how I feel about people truly learning their authority as Christ gave many examples. We need to follow in His footsteps in order to walk in the same health as he and his disciples did (and those today that know their authority).

I have been successful in taking my authority in Christ over all sickness and disease in my personal life since June of 2009. It has truly been amazing for me to live in the spirit of Christ and knowing that "by His stripes I was healed." I was tested along the way with various pains and symptoms but I persevered through all and was healed of all every time even though in some cases it looked really bad in the physical (having a painful golf ball sized something on the spine of my back is not something that I liked to have for seven weeks). I have proven to myself that by having faith to believe even though it was not easy, I could have given up too early and not seen Jesus heal me. This would have caused me to believe that sometimes he just cannot or will not heal for some reason. It would have sounded unbelievable to me just seven years ago to never need to take any Tylenol or ibuprofen for any pains, but that is exactly what I have seen in my personal life.

I used to have headaches at least ten times a year or more, but now I never have them. I also no longer take any food supplements or vitamins as the Lord said he would be my health provider so why waste my money on it. Good point Lord. My faith for healing changed from the vitamins and supplements that I used to take to the Lord and the Word and what they say. I have also changed my diet from eating fatty and fried foods to healthier foods such as fruits and vegetables and spinach salad. I often eat chicken, turkey and some types of fish and will occasionally have beef and pork without any concern. I rarely eat any processed sugars and will never drink any soft drinks because there is nothing good about them. I am not afraid of gluten or anything else that is the latest food craze and I enjoy bread and carbohydrates. Keep in mind that the enemy can also bring people into fear over what they eat if they do not know their authority and then they are in bondage. I have known several people that have been told they cannot eat this food or that food and are allergic to this or that. Until they truly know their authority of who they are in Christ, they may not be set free from the bondage of being allergic to various foods or airborne things. It is truly a good thing to have freedom to eat whatever you want (obviously if you eat junk all day you will gain weight and develop a host of challenges from that so you do need to have common sense). Just keep in mind what Jesus and the disciples ate (lots of fish and fruits and vegetables and bread).

Exercising is also important as everyone should go for at least a 30 minute or more walk a day and more vigorous workout if they can. I work out with weights on my upper body three times a week and lower body three times a week for about 45 minutes a day resting on Sundays. I also do cardio workouts six times a week using either an elliptical machine or treadmill or just run or walk. I feel so amazing after I exercise and feel like I am 20 years old in energy and health although I am actually 49 at the time I am writing this book. Walking in the authority of Christ makes all the difference in the world as you are never in fear ever of anything and always at peace knowing that God will provide and protect.

I have not had any health care insurance since I left my job with Intuit Financial Services in September of 2012 and have had no worry or fear for even 1 minute since. I know for many that would terrify you and it would have for me back in 2009 but since I have learned my authority it has not been a concern at all as I trust in the Lord and He is my healer. I was just thinking how much money I saved on not having it and not needing it and after I added it up the savings were many thousands of dollars. So please press in and spend time in your Bible and watching videos and listening to CD's and learning about your authority in Christ. I would recommend reading the book that has sold over 2 million copies (and probably more like 3 million now) called *The Believers Authority* by Kenneth E. Hagin.

Hagin talked about a man traveling with him for several months who was diabetic and previously had issues with his blood sugar. Interestingly when the man traveled with Hagin he never tested for any issues with his blood sugar. One night Hagin told him to eat a piece of pie and said that the man would not test for any increase in sugar in his blood because of the strong anointing that was on Hagin as that would protect the man's own challenges in his faith for knowing his authority. The man did not believe Hagin so he ate the piece of pie and when he went back to his room he tested his blood and it came up perfectly normal. He could not believe it. The whole time he was with Hagin his blood sugar tested normally. Then after Hagin left him, within days the man started seeing issues with his blood once again because he never truly knew his authority as a believer for himself. It took the man over a year before he finally learned his authority in Christ and never had an issue again.

Hagin also mentions in the book that when he first married his wife she used to always get sick in the fall and had to have her throat swabbed in order to get healthy. When Hagin learned his authority his wife no longer became sick every fall. I would encourage you to review three videos that were recorded of Hagin talking about *The Believer's Authority* on YouTube as he does a great job talking about and explaining authority and gives many examples that are not in his book. Hagin also talked about a time when he was driving with his family out West and it was late at night many miles from the next town with no gas station in sight. His gas gauge read empty so he just declared to his car "You will get me to the next town without stopping" and sure enough they drove for another hour with no gas and upon arriving in town and stopping at a gas station Hagin's son remembered getting out and trying to smell gas fumes from opening up the gas cap and could not smell any at all. It was an extraordinary display of taking authority over any situation.

Hagin explains: The door to exercising authority pivots upon two phrases Paul prayed for the Ephesians: "...and set him at his own right hand in the heavenly places" (Eph. 1:20), and "...hath raised us up together" (Eph. 2:6).

Meditate on these two prayers. Learn to pray them for yourself. Feed on their truths until they become a part of your inner consciousness. Then they will dominate your life. Don't try to accept them mentally; you've got to get the revelation of them in your spirit – and that is much harder – to truly understand it in your spirit which is knowing without a shadow of a doubt.

Notice that not only is Christ seated at the right hand of the Father, above all the powers in Satan's realm, but we are there, too, because God "hath raised us up together." Not only have we been made to sit, but notice where we are sitting: "Far above all principality, and power, and might, and dominion...." (Eph. 1:21).

In the mind of God, we were raised when Christ was raised. When Christ sat down, we sat down, too. That's where we are now, positionally speaking: We're seated at the right hand of the Father with Christ. (The act of Christ being seated implies that, for the time being, at least, certain aspects of His work are suspended.)

All the authority that was given to Christ belongs to us through Him, and we may exercise it. We help Him by carrying out His work upon the earth. And one aspect of His work that the Word of God tells us to do is to conquer the devil! In fact, Christ cannot do His work on the earth without us!

Someone will argue, "Well, He can get along without me, but I need Him." No, He cannot get along without you any more than you can get along without Him. You see, the truth that Paul is bringing out here in Ephesians is that Christ is the Head and we are the Body.

What if your body said, "I can get along without the head. I don't need my head." No, your body cannot get along without your head. And what if your head said, "Well, I can get along without my body. I don't need it; I can get along without heart and lungs." No, actually you cannot.

Likewise, Christ cannot get along without us, because the work of Christ and God is carried out through the Body of Christ. His work never will be done apart from us—and we never can get along without Him.

Ephesians 6:12 says, "For we wrestle not against flesh and blood, but against principalities, against powers...." If you take this verse out of its setting and go on talking about this awful fight we're in against the devil and describing how powerful the devil is, you've missed the whole point Paul was making—because that's not what he's saying in Ephesians.

Remember, when Paul wrote this letter to the Church at Ephesus, he didn't divide it into chapters and verses. Scholars did that at a much later date to help us in making reference. You can do great harm sometimes by picking one verse out of a chapter, taking it out of its setting, and making it say something it doesn't say (torturing or twisting scripture).

The Holy Spirit through Paul already has said in the second chapter that we are seated above these powers that we have to deal with. Not only is Christ seated at the right hand of the Father, far above all these powers, but we're there, too, because God has made us sit together with Christ.

Therefore, in our battle against the enemy and his forces, we need to keep in mind that we are above them and we have authority over them. The Word tells us that Jesus has **already** conquered them. Our job is to enforce His victory. His victory belongs to us, but we are to carry it out.

What I really appreciate about Hagin is that he understood the revelation of his authority in Christ. He knew what it meant and was very good at articulating it to others and then training people all over the world to walk in it and do what Jesus did, healing the sick, casting out demons and loving on hurting people. When you truly learn your authority in Christ it is a life and game changer. It changes everything and is the greatest feeling in the world to know you are now a dangerous, fully equipped warrior for the Lord against the enemy. Otherwise what kind of Christian are you? I lived both ways and experienced what it was like to not know my authority. It did not serve me well. When I did not know my authority I walked around trying to convince people to become Christians so they could go to heaven. But what good is it if you are in just as much sickness and pain and depression as all the non-believers? What was the selling point to convince someone to become a Christian for their remaining time on earth? I used to be a sales executive and if you could not come up with a compelling reason to get someone to choose what you were selling you would not get the sale. So tell me – what is your compelling reason to sell Christ to an unbeliever if they do not have any more than a promise that when they die they can spend eternity with Christ in heaven instead of hell yet must live on earth in being defeated by the enemy in their health, finances and relationships. What is different about their lives on earth until they get to heaven? They want to know what makes you different today!

When you show them that they can pray for people and get them healed just like Jesus did they get excited! They do not want to walk around in sickness like others for their remaining years and I do not blame them.

I remember when I was praying for a 70 something year old woman in her home in Carmel who had never been healed before of anything. Her daughter asked if I could pray for her and she said "sure" not really expecting to be healed from anything. This is the usual challenge I have to deal with because so many people never see anyone receive healing because those praying for them do not know how to pray and do not know their authority. I explained to her some of the healings that I had seen because I learned to pray more effectively and her faith began to raise a little to an expectation to be healed instantly – not eventually or not at all as she was used to seeing. So she told me her hip had been giving her a lot of pain and she felt she had a pinched nerve for over a week. I had her sit down so I could check the length of her legs. One leg was a little shorter than the other so I commanded it to grow and out it did. The look on her face was one of surprise. Then as she was sitting down I spoke to the pain in her hip and instantly it left and she started to have tears come from her eyes. I love seeing that because I know the Holy Spirit was drawing her to the Lord in a real and tangible way. She got up and walked around with all pain gone. So then her faith started to really rise and she said "I also have hard nodules on my thyroid and neck" so I put my hands on her neck and said "Thyroid be healed, nodules dissolve in Jesus name" and instantly she felt heat and the nodules dissolving. Now she was ecstatic and so thankful to the realness of what Jesus was doing. Then the Lord gave me a word of knowledge and told her that her back and neck and posture needed corrected so she stood up. Then I commanded her back and posture to be healed and made perfect and gently she felt her posture straighten up and her shoulders come back into perfect position and she knew it was the Lord. Now she felt goosebumps all over her arms and body and heat. The Holy Spirit was now overwhelming her and she had no doubt that what just happened was the most amazing, crazy, real display of love from the Lord. Healing is something you can all do but only if you really know that you carry the same authority as Christ and when you command you expect to see the same results. Now that is what Jesus was expecting all Christians to do. This is what is missing in the church today! There are too many dead churches that never see any healings and when people pray no one gets healed because they pray asking God to heal when He already gave it to you to do over 2,000 years ago when Jesus died on the cross.

Andrew Wommack lives in Colorado and has a growing ministry of teaching people to live their lives more like Christ with love and grace and knowing their authority in Christ. He also wrote many books including one called *The Believer's Authority*. Wommack has posted free TV shows archived on his website that allow you to watch about the believer's authority. Andrew had given me a prophetic word about my future ministry as he said that it would touch the lives of thousands and thousands of people and would involve deliverance, prophetic words, healing and teaching. Andrew is the most down to earth, matter of fact speaker you will ever hear. He had a powerful deliverance and healing ministry when he lived in Texas and now has a great teaching ministry and Bible school raising up people full of faith around the world who know their authority in Christ.

Wommack has a testimony similar to my back story (when my back popped out and I was in extreme pain for two days) when he was working on a garage door and his back popped out and he was laid out on the driveway in severe pain. He was supposed to be ordained as a pastor the next day and decided that in order to be healed he needed to exercise his faith. So he was in very strong pain for the first day and even by the second day he was still in pain. It was not until he got in the car and was on his way to the ordination event that he finally became healed as he would not give up and give in to the enemy.

Wommack had a son named Peter that died on March 4, 2001 and it took him seventy five minutes from the time he received the call his son was dead until he was able to drive into town and arrive at the hospital. He knew that there were many prophecies that had not yet been fulfilled so he declared that his son would not die but live. By the time he arrived at the hospital his son was sitting up and alive again. Knowing your authority can be a life or death situation.

Above is a picture with me and Andrew Wommack when we connected in August of 2013 in Chicago.

Earlier in my book I had mentioned that when I read about the life of John G. Lake that I wanted to have my own Healing Rooms someday. John G. Lake opened the first Healing Room in Spokane in 1915 and eventually had it in operation six days a week. He also opened them up in other places like Portland and up and down the California coast and started many churches that had healing rooms. He saw so many healings that according to statistics the U.S. Government declared Spokane to be the 'Healthiest City in America'. He used to see a very high percent of healings and for those that did not get healed instantly he had them stay and watch others get healed and learn about their authority and then normally within a couple of weeks they were healed as well. Lake would go to hospitals and heal patients and it got to where hospitals no longer had much need for the beds anymore. Doctors would refer their patients to him to receive healing. He was responsible for over 1 million converts, 100,000+ healings, 625 churches and 1,250 preachers in five years of ministry! The Bubonic plague caused the Black Death that swept through Asia, Europe and Africa in the 14th century and killed an estimated 50 million people which was about 50% of the population. Below is one testimony of John G. Lake when the Bubonic Plague was sweeping through where he lived in South Africa from 1908 to 1913. This is a great example of why it is so important to know your authority in Christ.

"Faith belongs to the law of life. **Faith is the very opposite of fear** *(emphasis added). Faith has the opposite effect in spirit, soul, and body. Faith causes the spirit of man to become confident. It causes the mind of man to become restful, and positive. A positive mind repels disease. Consequently, the emanation of the Spirit destroys disease germs.*

And because we were in contact with the Spirit of life, I and a little Dutch fellow with me went out and buried many of the people who had died from the bubonic plague. We went into the homes and carried them out, dug the graves and put them in. Sometimes we would put three or four in one grave.

We never took the disease. Why? Because of the knowledge that the law of life in Christ Jesus protects us. That law was working. Because of the fact that a man by that action of his will, puts himself purposely in contact with God, faith takes possession of his heart, and the condition of his nature is changed. Instead of being fearful, he is full of faith. Instead of being absorbent and drawing everything to himself, his spirit repels sickness and disease. The Spirit of Christ Jesus flows through the whole being, and emanates through the hands, the heart, and from every pore of the body.

During that great plague that I mentioned, they sent a government ship with supplies and corps of doctors. One of the doctors sent for me, and said, "What have you been using to protect yourself? Our corps has this preventative and that, which we use as protection, but we concluded that if a man could stay on the ground as you have and keep ministering to the sick and burying the dead, you must have a secret. What is it?"

I answered, "Brother that is the 'law of the Spirit of life in Christ Jesus'. I believe that just as long as I keep my soul in contact with the living God so that His Spirit is flowing into my soul and body, that no germ will ever attach itself to me, for the Spirit of God will kill it." He asked, "Don't you think that you had better use our preventatives?" I replied, "No, but doctor I think that you would like to experiment with me. If you will go over to one of these dead people and take the foam that comes out of their lungs after death, then put it under the microscope you will see masses of living germs. You will find they are alive until a reasonable time after a man is dead. You can fill my hand with them and I will keep it under the microscope and instead of these germs remaining alive, they will die instantly." They tried it and found it was true. They questioned, "What is that?" I replied, "That is the 'law of the Spirit of life in Christ Jesus.' When a man's spirit and a man's body are filled with the blessed presence of God, it oozes out of the pores of your flesh and kills the germs."

Suppose on the other hand, my soul had been under the law of death, and I were in fear and darkness? The very opposite would have been the result. The result would have been that my body would have absorbed the germs, these would have generated disease and I would have died.

You who are sick, put yourself in contact with God's law of life. Read His Word with the view of enlightening your heart so that you will be able to look up with more confidence and believe Him. Pray that the Spirit of God will come into your soul, take possession of your body, and its power will make you well. That is the exercise of the law of the Spirit of life in Christ Jesus."

This is a very real case of why it is so critically important to know your authority and as John G. Lake puts it "exercising of the law of the Spirit of life in Christ Jesus." How will you react when a new plague dujour comes into existence? Remember in 2014-15 when the Ebola crisis came from Africa to the United States? Everyone got into fear and worry as people and nurses were dying and there was no known cure for it. Fortunately I had no fear at any time because I knew that I could not get it because just like Lake it could not harm me because of my knowing that I was protected by Christ Jesus.

What is the next great scare that will cause panic and fear in the world? If you know your authority as a believer in Christ you would not need to have any fear as you would know that you would be protected. This is a life and death situation whether you would like to admit it or not. I would estimate that 99% of Christians have no clue about their authority in Christ when it comes to their health. If you know your authority in Christ you will live in perfect peace and faith at all times. If you do not know it you will live in fear, worry and pain. The perfect love of Christ Jesus casts out all fear. Hebrews 11:1 NKJV *says "Now faith is the substance of things hoped for, the evidence of things not seen."* and Hebrews 11:3 NKJV says *"By faith we understand that the worlds were framed by the words of God, so that the things which are seen were not made of things which are visible."* If God created the universe by speaking things into existence and then sent Jesus to earth to give man all power and authority over every sickness, disease and situation then why be afraid? But you must know that you know that you know your authority in Christ because the enemy <u>will know</u> if you know it or not.

A great example of this truth is in the book of Acts 19:13-16 NKJV *"13 Then some of the itinerant Jewish exorcists took it upon themselves to call the name of the Lord Jesus over those who had evil spirits, saying, "We exorcise you by the Jesus whom Paul preaches." 14 Also there were seven sons of Sceva, a Jewish chief priest, who did so.*
15 And the evil spirit answered and said, "Jesus I know, and Paul I know; but who are you?"
16 Then the man in whom the evil spirit was leaped on them, overpowered them, and prevailed against them, so that they fled out of that house naked and wounded."

God wants us to be healthy and live a productive life full of faith, miracles, signs and wonders. So go out there and live your life in faith, power and love – do not worry or fear for even a second as that is the only way the enemy can bring anything upon you. Walk every day of your life in power, authority and love, the same that Jesus Christ taught His disciples and you will see amazing things all the remaining days of your life.

References

Kenneth E. Hagin, *The Believer's Authority*
Andrew Wommack, *The Believer's Authority*
Maria Woodworth-Etter, *Signs & Wonders*
John G. Lake, *The Complete Collection of His Life Teachings*

Final Thoughts

The Lord has told me that everyone knows of many in their lives that are suffering from sickness and disease. Please make your family and friends aware that they can break the cycle of sickness and pain and take back control over their lives but they need to know their authority as a believer. There is great peace when you truly know that the enemy cannot hurt you but there is fear when you do not know.

If you would like me to speak or minister at your church, seminar or conference you may contact me on my website. If the revelations in this book have helped you and changed your life you may make a tax deductible donation to Restored to Freedom at www.restoredtofreedom.com which will help to continue to get the message to people all over the world that there is hope and a way to gain total freedom.

37962462R00077

Made in the USA
Middletown, DE
09 March 2019